# FAME & FLOW:

*The Real Alchemy of Brand Growth*

Initiative
100 West 33rd Street, New York 10001

Copyright © 2024 by Dimitri Maex & Jonathan Rigby
All rights reserved
Printed in the United States of America
Published in 2024 by Initiative
Maex, Dimitri & Rigby, Jonathan
Fame & Flow: The Real Alchemy of Brand Growth /
Dimitri Maex & Jonathan Rigby

ISBN: 9798340254528

Cover design by Jess Marques
Book layout by Brooke Palladino

*For Bruce, Ray, & Katherine Maex*
*For Leo & Dima Rigby*

# ABOUT THE AUTHORS

## DIMITRI MAEX

Dimitri Maex is the CEO of Global Media Agency Initiative, part of IPG. Dimitri has a background in media and data analytics, with extensive experience in managing creative agencies and a passion for strategy. Dimitri has held leadership roles at IPG, WPP and data science startup Sentiance. This is Maex's second book. The first one, "Sexy Little Numbers," was published by Crown Business and has been translated into six languages.

Born and raised in Antwerp, Belgium, Dimitri studied econometrics at the University of Antwerp and got his MBA at the Xavier Institute of Management in Bhubaneswar-India. He lives in Katonah, NY with his wife Katherine and their children Ray and Bruce.

## JONATHAN RIGBY

Jonathan Rigby is Initiative's Global Chief Strategy Officer, where he oversees a team tasked with making brands more relevant in consumers' lives.

Jonathan started out in WPP's Fellowship Program and has honed his craft in brand research, planning, media, and performance at powerhouse agencies including Kantar, Ogilvy, and Digitas in London, Hong Kong, and New York.

He currently calls Brooklyn home with his wife Dima, son Leo, and a mess of bikes, tents, wetsuits, Gore-Tex, and assorted toddler toys, trying to align nap schedules to outdoor adventures.

# FAME & FLOW
*The Real Alchemy of Brand Growth*

## TABLE OF CONTENTS

**PREFACE** .................................................................................................. IV

**CHAPTER 1 – HOUSTON WE HAVE A PROBLEM** ........................................ 1

Trapped In Pixels ......................................................................................... 2

The New Gods Of Numbers ........................................................................ 5

The High Priests of the Algorithm .............................................................. 8

The Illusion of a Formula .......................................................................... 11

The Truman Show of Marketing ............................................................... 13

The Boardroom's Comfort Zone ............................................................... 15

**CHAPTER 2 – A NEW MENTAL MODEL FOR MARKETING** ...................... 18

How Does Marketing Work, Really? ......................................................... 19

Mental Models - A B2B Example .............................................................. 23

Mental Models - An Example from the Gut ............................................. 26

Fame and Flow: The New Creed of Marketing ........................................ 28

Fame: The Neon Glow in the Market's Dark Alley ................................... 30

The Algebra of the Air: Calculating the Fame Quotient .......................... 32

The Numbers that Sing: The Business Ballad of Fame ............................ 35

Defining Fame Beyond the Eyeballs ......................................................... 37

The F-Factors: Sketching the Anatomy of Fame ...................................... 40

The Dance of Flow: Beyond the Limelight to the Checkout Line ........... 43

Navigating the Currents of Flow: The Tangibility of Availability ............ 45

The Precision of Persuasion: Timing & Message in the Dance of Desire ............. 47

The F-Factors: Defining the Currents of Flow.......................................................... 49

**CHAPTER 3 – DISSECTING FAME & FLOW** .................................................51

Familiarity: The Foundation of Fame ........................................................................ 52

Favorability: The Delicate Dance of Likability & Preference ................................ 58

Feeling & the Power of Distinctive Media Assets.................................................... 64

Fervor: The Wildfire of Word-of-Mouth .................................................................. 72

Findability: Navigating the Digital & Physical Realms ........................................ 78

Facilitation: Smoothing the Path to Purchase ......................................................... 84

Fascination: The Art of Capturing Hearts & Minds ............................................... 92

Following: Building Bonds That Last ........................................................................ 99

Fame x Flow: The Twin Engines of Growth .......................................................... 105

**CHAPTER 4 – BUILDING FAME & FLOW** ................................................... 110

Crafting Your Fame & Flow Blueprint ................................................................... 111

Diagnosing Fame & Flow: The First Critical Step................................................. 113

The Fame & Flow Audit: Unveiling the Story Behind the Scores ...................... 118

Prioritization: The Art of Selective Focus in Fame & Flow................................. 121

**CHAPTER 5 – FAME & FLOW AS A CHANGE AGENT** ........................... 123

Breathing New Life into an Old Concept: Integration ........................................ 124

Simplify, Simplify, Simplify ...................................................................................... 127

Never-ending Experimentation: Constantly x Consistently............................... 130

**CLOSING TIME** .................................................................................................. 133

**APPENDIX – DETAILED RESEARCH FINDINGS** ..................................... 137

**INDEX**.................................................................................................................... 150

# PREFACE

This isn't just a book; it's a manifesto, a battle cry from the depths of Initiative, where we've been stewing and brewing over how marketing really ticks. Over the last two years, we've torn apart old beliefs and poked at the bloated egos of outdated marketing models with a sharp stick. What we found needed a voice, a loud, unapologetic voice that could only be echoed through the clacking keys of a typewriter that smelled of late nights. This is the culmination of endless conversations about what makes marketing work. It's about cutting through the noise and getting to the marrow of what it means to connect with humanity on a level that isn't just about selling, but about creating something memorable, something lasting.

Initiative isn't just any agency. It's a place where creativity meets data on a blind date and decides to dance until the sun comes up. We owe a mountain of thanks to the thousands of souls at Initiative worldwide. Every day, you are out there building Fame and Flow for our clients, weaving narratives that don't just exist but live, breathe, and resonate across the globe. You are the lifeblood of this agency, and every page of this book is infused with your spirit and dedication.

To our clients, those titans of industry who trust us with the keys to their kingdoms, thank you for letting us play in your sandboxes, for daring to walk the edge with us. This journey is yours as much as it is ours.

A special thanks goes to Annie Perretta, whose prowess in research and content helped shape the substance of our story. To Jim Dravillas and the KINESSO team, whose diligent stewardship of the research and development of diagnostic tools allowed us to measure what we once merely mused upon. Katy Varner, your analytical mind has been the compass guiding us through data-driven storms. Ben Richards, Faris Yakob, and The Intangibles, your insights and provocations have helped us shape our worldview and refine our offerings to something beyond the ordinary. Willa Robertson, Paolo Sarno, and Ilana Orlansky, your efforts in launching this book have been nothing short of heroic.

And let's not forget our AI companion, whose ability to churn out prose with the grime and grit of dirty realism brought an authentic voice to our narrative. This was an interesting experiment, a testament to the marriage of machine learning and human creativity, pushing the boundaries of what technology can do when guided by human touch.

We wanted a book with attitude, one that doesn't just sit comfortably on the shelf but stands out, disrupts, and demands attention. This journey has been as much about rediscovering the art of marketing as it has been about defining its science. It's about finding balance in the binaries—data and desire, analytics and creativity, reach and resonance.

As you turn these pages, you'll find not just the fruits of our labor but an invitation. An invitation to rethink, to challenge, and to ultimately understand the dual forces of Fame and Flow. This book isn't just about what we've learned—it's about learning to look at marketing not just as a function of business but as a feature of human interaction.

With "Fame & Flow," we offer not just insights but a lens through which to view the landscape of consumer engagement anew. To our fellow marketers, to our esteemed clients, and to anyone who believes in the power of a good story: may this book light your way as we all navigate the nuanced narratives of brand growth in the digital age.

*Let the journey begin.*

## CHAPTER 1

# HOUSTON, WE HAVE A PROBLEM

## *Trapped In Pixels*

In the fluorescent haze of modernity, where the glow of screens outshines the sun, we've stumbled into a quandary, clad in pixels and paranoia. The pixel, that smallest dot on a digital canvas, and the cookie, a crumb left behind in every corner of the cyber world, became the tools of an era—though nobody asked if they should. These little digital bastards crept into the marketing world like a virus slips into blood, silent and undetected until the fever hits.

The history of these tiny tyrants is as mundane as it is revolutionary. The pixel originated in the pixelated mind of computer scientist Robert Kirsch in 1957. Initially designed to render digital images on computer screens, pixels became the basic unit of digital measurement, a way to break the world into digestible, digital bites.

Then came the cookie, a seemingly innocuous invention by a web programmer in the early 90s, intended to remember you by your digital footsteps. It was meant to be a convenience, storing details like login information so you wouldn't have to trek through the same questions every time you ventured onto a website. But soon, it mutated into a tool for persistent, invasive tracking, a way for marketers to follow you home, sit on your couch, and watch what you eat for dinner.

As these tools proliferated, they wove themselves into the very fabric of marketing strategies, becoming as indispensable as the air marketers breathed. They underpinned an entire ecosystem that evolved rapidly over the last two decades—a behemoth of ad tech sprawling its tentacles through the digital world, clutching every touchpoint of consumer interaction. This ecosystem promised nirvana: total visibility, complete control, perfect knowledge of where every dollar went and what it brought back.

Digital marketers wielded these tools like modern sorcerers, conjuring sales and conversions with a few keystrokes, their screens lit with the cold glow of dashboards filled with metrics—clicks, impressions, conversions. Each campaign became a calculated affair, each strategy a series of algorithmic adjustments. The art of marketing, the human touch, the intuition and gut feeling that once guided campaigns were sidelined, dismissed as relics of an unenlightened past.

But this obsession with metrics, with quantifiable outcomes, with the measurable and the manageable, began to cast a long shadow. The bigger picture of how marketing really works—how it resonates with the messy, irrational human psyche—started to blur. The focus narrowed, drilling down into data points, losing sight of the landscape. Marketing, in its essence, is about connection, emotion, about feeling your way through the desires and dreams of the audience. Yet, in the sterile light of digital dashboards, these subtleties often faded into the background.

CMOs, those captains of the industry, found themselves steered by stars that had been realigned by digital decree. They navigated by charts that told them everything about where a consumer clicked but nothing about why; everything about the journey but nothing about the experience. And as they sailed these digital seas, the very essence of marketing—the human connection—was left adrift.

This crisis, this myopia, is not just a problem; it's a symptom of a deeper malaise—a fixation with the visible and the immediate, at the expense of the enduring and profound. The tools that should have been servants became masters, dictating strategies that churned out optimized mediocrity, campaigns that reverberated in the echo chambers of the internet, but seldom touched the heart or moved the spirit.

As the digital metrics continue to pour in, filling spreadsheets and reports, the question looms large: Are we, the marketers, losing our way? Are we mistaking the map for the territory, the medium for the message, the metrics for the meaning?

This is a call to those who care not just for the mechanics of marketing but for its soul, to those who dare to look beyond the pixels and the cookies, to see the vast, uncharted human landscape that lies beyond the reach of any dashboard. It's time to step back, to look up from the screens, and to see the forest for the trees.

## *The New Gods Of Numbers*

Not long so ago, when letters actually hit mailboxes and salespeople dirtied their shoes on front doorsteps, there was a kind of rugged poetry. It was direct marketing—straightforward, no-nonsense, a punch to the gut. You knew when it hit because you heard the thud of the impact. Then, as the digital age crept up like dawn over the hill of progress, everything got a shot of steroids, including marketing. The hard knocks turned into silent clicks, and direct mail morphed into performance marketing, worshiping at the altar of immediacy and accuracy.

The shift wasn't subtle; it was a revolution painted in code and clicks. The direct marketing strategies of the past—mailers that could be touched and tossed, calls that echoed in empty houses—transformed under the influence of new digital technologies. The cookie and the pixel, those tiny dictators of the digital realm, gave marketers a way to see in real-time how their campaigns fared without waiting for the mail to be sorted or the phone to ring.

Performance marketing emerged from this union of old-school tactics and new-world tech, its heart beating in time with each click-through rate. It was direct marketing reborn, reimagined, and reinvigorated. It wasn't about reaching out to feel the pulse of the potential customer anymore; it was about tracking that pulse through data streams, understanding desires and decisions without ever seeing a face or hearing a voice.

The charm of performance marketing was its promise of accountability. Every click had a backstory, every sale a digital footprint, leading marketers to tweak their campaigns with surgical precision. And the platforms—Google and Meta—they got fat on this new creed. They built empires on algorithms, auctioning visibility to the highest bidder and promising unparalleled access to the eyeballs of millions. The game was fast, relentless, and intoxicatingly measurable.

Marketers, in their rush to capitalize on this new playground, started to operate like traders on the floor of the stock exchange. The language of marketing shifted—it was all about conversions, CPM, CPC, CPA, and other acronyms that sounded like military code but were just ways to measure the cost of buying human attention. Budgets ballooned in digital spaces as boardrooms nodded along, enamored with spreadsheets that showed clear lines from spend to revenue.

Yet, for all its dazzle, performance marketing began to show its seams, fraying at the edges. The focus on immediate results started cannibalizing the future. Brands became fixated on the next click, the next conversion, at the expense of building lasting relationships with their consumers. The narrative depth of traditional advertising—the story that built emotional connections—was often lost in the noise of transactional exchanges.

What's more, the environment this created was frenetic and fickle. Consumer loyalty, once the holy grail of brand equity, became as transient as a page view. Campaigns were optimized to exhaustion, each iteration shaving margins finer and finer, in an endless loop of testing and targeting.

As the dust kicked up by this frenzy began to settle, a question hung in the air, heavy and uncomfortable: What had been lost in this mad dash for measurable outcomes? Had the essence of marketing—the human connection, the craft of storytelling—been traded for a dashboard of analytics? Performance marketing had promised a revolution, but as the cracks began to widen, it seemed it might just as well presage a reckoning.

In the harsh glare of retargeted ads and SEO-optimized content, the marketers started to wonder if perhaps they had gone too far. As performance marketing matured, it became clear that it was not just a tool but a lens—and one that could distort as much as it clarified. The challenge now was not just how to use this lens, but how to correct for its deformations.

### *The High Priests of the Algorithm*

The digital world has its overlords—Meta and Google. They reign supreme, their thrones built on data, their scepters wired with algorithms. As performance marketing soared, these giants didn't just ride the wave; they directed its course, making every click, every view, every fleeting online interaction not just trackable but monetizable. They became the puppeteers, and the digital marketers? Just strings to be pulled.

These platforms, with their sprawling, omnipotent reach, transformed marketing from a craft to a science—a cold, hard science of algorithms and analytics where every transaction was scrutinized under the digital microscope. They sold certainty in an uncertain world. Need to drive sales? Click here. Want to boost engagement? Click there. It was all laid out in dashboards that glittered like the Las Vegas strip, seducing CMOs with dazzling displays of efficiency and effectiveness.

But beneath this shiny surface, a more complex and darker narrative played out. Meta and Google weren't just servicing the marketing world; they were molding it in their image. With every algorithm update, they nudged the behaviors of millions, directing traffic and attention with the finesse of a casino owner who knows the house must always win. Their algorithms became black boxes—mysterious, proprietary, and designed to maximize not just the ROI for advertisers but their own bottom lines.

As these algorithms evolved, they began to automate more and more of the decision-making process. What started as a tool for marketers to use at their discretion became an essential crutch. Meta and Google pitched it as liberation from the drudgery of micromanagement, a way for creative minds to free themselves from the banality of bidding and budget adjustments. But this 'liberation' was a gilded cage. Marketers fed their budgets into these digital behemoths and watched the autopilot navigate, rarely questioning where it was headed or at what cost.

These platforms claimed to optimize marketing spends towards business outcomes, but the underlying tune was different. The algorithms were finely tuned to maximize engagement—and engagement meant revenue, not just for the advertisers but even more so for the platforms themselves. As Meta and Google grew richer, bloated on the vast influx of ad dollars, the marketplace became distorted, a funhouse mirror reflecting not the needs of the consumers but the algorithms' insatiable hunger for more data, more clicks, more of the lifeblood of the digital age.

CMOs watched these developments with a mix of awe and dependency. The dashboards provided by these platforms offered a mesmerizing insight into the journey of every dollar spent, tracing its path from impression to conversion. But this granular visibility was a double-edged sword. Yes, they could see everything—but through a lens crafted by the very entities that profited from their spend. They were under the illusion of control, but it was the algorithms that pulled the strings, subtly shaping the landscape of digital marketing to suit their creators' ends.

And so, the noose tightened. With each passing quarter, the digital marketing realm moved further from human intuition and closer to algorithmic determinism. Marketers found themselves riding a train they no longer drove, barreling down tracks laid by corporations whose interests were aligned not with the brands they served but with their own exponential growth.

The question then arose, murmured in conference rooms and whispered in webinars: What happens when the algorithms know your customers better than you do? What happens when they don't just suggest strategies but dictate them? In this new world, marketers were left to wonder—were they still masters of their fate, or had they become mere variables in an equation written in Silicon Valley? As the digital dusk grew darker, the industry faced a reckoning: to reclaim their role or continue to be pawns in a game ruled by algorithms.

## *The Illusion of a Formula*

In the smudged, worn edges of the marketing world, a ghost lingers—the ghost of Claude Hopkins, whose book "Scientific Advertising," penned in the roaring twenties, heralded a future where marketing would be as precise as physics. The past two decades of performance marketing, fueled by algorithms and data, seemed to have finally sculpted that dream into stark reality.

It was Hopkins who first imagined marketing stripped of its guesswork, a discipline where every decision, from copy to placement, was guided by hard data. The digital age, with its relentless tracking, targeting, and testing, has ostensibly turned this vision into a daily routine for marketers across the globe. Here, in this brave new world, every ad impression, every click and conversion, is measured with the precision of a lab experiment. Marketing, the art of persuasion, has seemingly morphed into a science.

But scratch the surface, and the sheen begins to dull. The digital revolution promised clarity but often delivered complexity. The data streams are endless, the dashboards dizzying. Marketers sit before screens dotted with metrics, each number a pulse point of consumer behavior, each dataset a roadmap to riches. The modern marketing department resembles a NASA control room more than a Madison Avenue brainstorm session. There's a sense of control, of mastery over the markets—until there isn't.

For what are these numbers, really? Can the sum of clicks and impressions truly capture the whims of human desire, the subtleties of taste, or the sway of culture? Hopkins' world was black and white; ours is a blur of gray. The algorithms promise precision, but they often peddle probabilities. The model says one thing; the market, another. The science of marketing, it turns out, isn't so scientific after all.

And what of the customer—the living, breathing human on the other side of the screen? In the rush to quantify everything, to reduce people to pixels, have marketers lost sight of the unquantifiable? Emotions, dreams, the spontaneous joy of discovery—these are the elements that no cookie can track, no pixel can capture.

The allure of a completely scientific marketing approach is powerful. It offers the illusion of certainty in an uncertain world. But it's just that— an illusion. The data may tell us how many, how much, and how often, but it struggles to explain why. It can guide a customer to a checkout page, but it can't make them feel at home there.

This is the paradox at the heart of the performance marketing revolution. For all its advancements, for all its precision, it leaves unanswered the most human questions. Claude Hopkins envisioned a world where advertising was a science, but science has its limits, especially when applied to the messy reality of human lives.

As marketers, we must ask ourselves: In our quest for certainty, what have we overlooked? What have we sacrificed? The answers may lead us to a deeper understanding of what marketing can and cannot be—a field guided by data but defined by humanity. In the pursuit of scientific advertising, we must remember that our ultimate aim is not to perfect the algorithm, but to connect with the human.

## *The Truman Show of Marketing*

They sit, eyes glued to screens that blink back at them in cool, serene detachment. The screens are their world, their universe, meticulously constructed with the precision of a painter's brush—only the paint is data, and the canvas is digital. Today's marketers, much like Truman from that old movie *The Truman Show*, wander through a reality meticulously orchestrated by higher powers. They live in a simulation crafted not of brick and mortar, but of pixels and click-through rates, built not by a director named Christof, but by the almighty giants of Silicon Valley—Google and Meta.

In Truman's world, every corner of his life was monitored, manipulated, and manufactured for the entertainment of unseen viewers, with Truman none the wiser. Similarly, marketers seem to operate within parameters set by the big platforms, their every decision influenced, nudged, or outright dictated by algorithms they neither fully understand nor control. These platforms shape the world of marketing with the subtlety of puppeteers, crafting what appears to be a seamless reality but is, in truth, an illusion.

Like Truman, who slowly realizes that his world is but a set, CMOs too need to awaken to the realization that the neat, quantifiable universe of performance marketing is a construct. It's a set built for them to play on, where the scripts are written by software engineers rather than screenwriters. But real marketing, much like real life, is messy, unpredictable, and beautifully irrational.

The true role of a CMO should not be confined to analyzing data trails left by consumers; it should be about venturing beyond the confines of this digital dome. Real CMOs need to be explorers, philosophers, rebels. They need to be curious—not just about what the data tells them, but about what it doesn't. They need to question every assumption, challenge every statistic, and look for the stories behind the numbers.

Marketing is more than a science. It's an art, a dance between the company and its customers. It's about understanding not just how many people clicked on an ad, but why they felt compelled to do so. It's about seeing the person behind the purchase, the human behind the transaction. This requires a kind of bravery, a willingness to step off the meticulously crafted set and into the real world, where the script is unwritten and outcomes are unknown.

To truly excel, to truly see, CMOs must channel their inner Truman at the moment of his epiphany. They must push against the edges of their constructed reality, question the authenticity of every pixelated shadow, and dare to breach the boundaries set by their digital overlords. Only by doing so can they escape the spectacle, step off the set, and find themselves in the messy, glorious reality of genuine human engagement.

As the dawn breaks over this realization, perhaps then the marketing world can begin to shift—from a Truman Show of digital illusions to a genuine exploration of what makes us human.

## *The Boardroom's Comfort Zone*

In boardrooms around the world, where corporate chess is played, the kings and queens of business convene, their moves calculated with surgical precision. CMOs navigate a treacherous path here. They tread a fine line between the discernible metrics demanded by their boards and the nebulous human truths that govern consumer behavior. Herein lies the great illusion of control, a mirage in the desert of modern marketing.

For most corporate boards, the allure of treating marketing as a science—a field ripe for quantification and analysis—is irresistible. This perspective aligns neatly with their experience on the supply side of business, a realm they can manipulate with precision. Here, inputs and outputs are clear; invest in a machine, see your productivity rise. The metrics are straightforward, comforting in their predictability.

Yet the demand side, where marketing plays, operates under different rules. It is a domain ruled by consumers whose behaviors are anything but predictable. In this world, cause and effect wear veils of ambiguity, and the reactions to marketing stimuli are colored by a spectrum of psychological and social factors that resist simple quantification.

Understanding what happens on the demand side—the art of marketing effectiveness—is not about discovering absolute rules but about exploring a landscape where cause and effect are loosely, sometimes bizarrely, connected. Marketers delve into how we process information, how external perceptions or the opinions of our peers shape our views, how our behaviors align (or don't) with our internal narratives, and how today's thoughts on a brand might ripple out into tomorrow's choices. This is a world of relative unknowns, and the tools of marketing measurement and analysis aim not to dispel this uncertainty but to map it more clearly, to navigate it with a bit more confidence.

The corporate insistence on translating the fluid art of marketing into the rigid language of financial metrics has steered CMOs down a precarious path. By applying supply-side financial techniques to the demand side's complexities, we distort the very nature of marketing. We reduce a symphony to a series of notes that can be turned on and off at will, ignoring the fact that the music of the market is composed in real time, with each consumer writing their part. Organizational theorist and professor Tim Ambler once noted that while financial metrics are important, they distort reality and provide the illusion of control, much like cannabis distorts perceptions while offering the illusion of insight.

This illusion is dangerous. It obscures the real workings of marketing, reducing it to a 'black box'—opaque, mysterious, but expected to deliver. It shields the uninitiated from the messy reality of consumer psychology, from the myriad external factors that influence buyer behavior, and from the long-term effects of brand perception.

The challenge for modern marketers is not just to navigate this complex landscape but to educate their peers about the inherent uncertainties of the demand side. They must argue for a recognition of marketing's unique role—not as a faucet to be turned on and off at will, but as a garden to be cultivated, with patience and an understanding that not every seed planted will flourish in predictable ways.

The challenge for today's CMOs is monumental. They must operate within the constraints of their boardrooms' expectations while pushing the boundaries of what those boardrooms understand. They must manage not just a brand but the expectations of those who see the brand as a line item on a balance sheet rather than as a living, breathing entity within a marketplace of human emotions.

To thrive, CMOs must become not just marketers but translators and educators, bridging the gap between the hard certainty of the supply side and the fluid uncertainties of the demand side. They must turn their boardrooms into classrooms, their metrics into stories, and their strategies into lessons on the human condition. Only then can they hope to lead their companies not just to profitability, but to relevance in a marketplace that values authenticity as much as it does efficiency.

# CHAPTER 2

# A NEW MENTAL MODEL FOR MARKETING

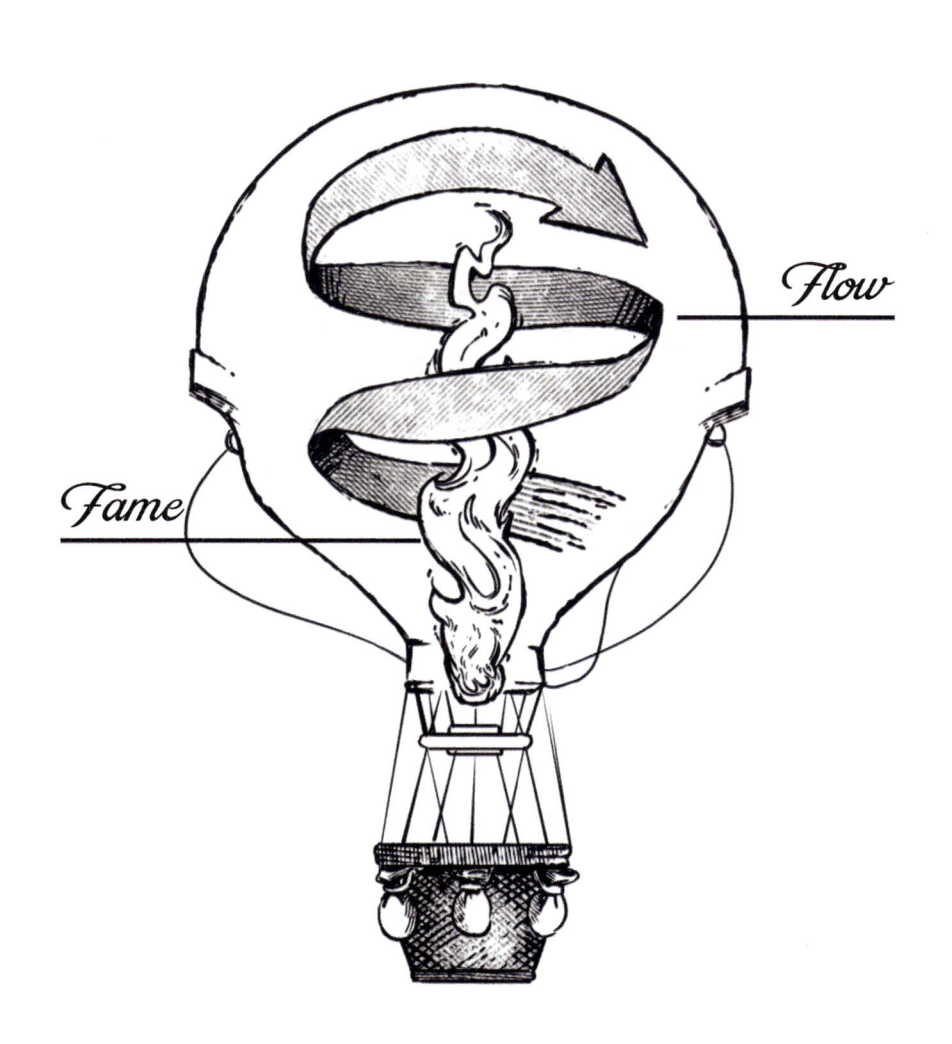

*Flow*

*Fame*

## How Does Marketing Work, Really?

Most CMOs are ill-prepared for taking on this mantle of educator and translator. This is because they often leap over a fundamental step: genuinely understanding how marketing works.

This understanding starts with developing a "mental model" for marketing, a conceptual framework that guides decisions and strategies. Yet, trapped in the labyrinth of outdated models like the marketing funnel, many CMOs continue to rely on an overly rational, simplified view of consumer decision-making. This traditional funnel, revered in textbooks and strategy sessions, glorifies a step-by-step consumer journey—from awareness to consideration to purchase—that rarely mirrors the chaotic, emotionally driven reality of the marketplace.

The funnel model fails miserably at acknowledging the messy human elements that critically influence buying decisions—emotions, peer influences, cultural undercurrents, and irrational behaviors. It's a neat diagram in a messy world, providing illusory comfort in predictability and control.

To break free from this outdated thinking, CMOs must first embrace the complexity of human behavior, recognizing that marketing is not a science to be neatly solved but an art to be continuously interpreted. Advertising expert Paul Feldwick, in his insightful book *Anatomy of Humbug*, outlines six distinct mental models for advertising that offer a broader perspective on how marketing can be approached:

**1. Advertising as Showmanship**—Inspired by P.T. Barnum's flamboyant tactics, this approach focuses on capturing attention by any means necessary. In modern contexts, it's the viral campaigns that create buzz through sheer spectacle or controversy, akin to State Street's Fearless Girl statue. While it risks veering into deception, at its best, it generates powerful, attention-grabbing narratives.

**2. Advertising as Salesmanship**—This method scales personal selling to a mass audience, employing clear, compelling messages that explain why a product is necessary. It's the realm of classic unique selling propositions (USPs). Geico's "15 minutes could save you 15% or more" commercials are a prime example, effectively differentiating Geico's products through direct, comparative advertising.

**3. Advertising as Seduction**—Here, the focus shifts from rational to emotional appeal, utilizing insights from social psychology to engage consumers on a deeper, more instinctual level. Nike's "Just Do It" and Dove's "Real Beauty" campaigns showcase how advertising can tap into aspirations and motivations, seducing consumers rather than just informing them.

**4. Advertising as Social Connection**—This modern theory sees advertising as creating a community or a shared sense of values among consumers. Airbnb's "Belong Anywhere" campaign or Red Bull's Extreme Sports Community exemplify how brands can forge emotional connections and loyalty through shared values and communal narratives.

**5. Advertising as Salience**—Based on Byron Sharp's principles in "How Brands Grow," this approach emphasizes the need for brands to be both mentally and physically available. It's about creating distinctive, memorable marketing that sticks in the consumer's mind. McDonald's "I'm loving it" campaign with its catchy jingle works this way. Budweiser's

"Wassup" is another example of a campaign that became a cultural phenomenon, embedding the brand in everyday greetings and making it top of mind in its category.

**6. Advertising as Spin**—Often used in politics, this method involves reframing the conversation to shift public perception. It's about changing the narrative to influence consumer sentiment and behavior subtly, demonstrating the power of perspective in shaping public opinion. Always' #LikeAGirl campaign did exactly that by empowering young girls and shifting the perception of doing something "like a girl" from an insult to a statement of confidence and capability.

For CMOs, the challenge is not just in selecting the right model but in crafting one that resonates with and is embraced by the entire organization. This mental model should not only encapsulate the nuances of modern marketing but also be simple enough to explain, robust enough to guide strategy, and flexible enough to adapt to new insights and market dynamics.

As marketing continues to evolve in an ever-more digital and data-driven landscape, the true task of the CMO is to guide their teams and companies through these complex waters with a mental model that acknowledges the art and science of the discipline. It's about recognizing that while data can illuminate parts of the puzzle, the broader picture is painted with strokes of human behavior, cultural shifts, and unpredictable market forces.

Thus, the first real step for any CMO or marketing leader is not to dive deeper into data but to step back and question the very foundations of their understanding of marketing. It's about challenging the status quo, pushing against the comfort of digital metrics, and embracing the messier, more human aspects of marketing that defy simple quantification. In doing so, they not only become better marketers but true leaders who can navigate the uncertain tides of consumer behavior with confidence and insight.

## *Mental Models - A B2B Example*

In the trenches of a Fortune 100 B2B tech company, marketing is a slow-burning fuse in a world obsessed with the instant sparks of sales achievements. Here, sales reign supreme, with every handshake and closed deal attributed to the charm and persistence of the sales team. Marketing, often viewed through a skeptical lens, struggles to showcase its impact amidst the long shadows cast by sales figures.

In this atmosphere, the company's CMO, tasked with defending the value of brand advertising, faced the relentless pressure of performance metrics that favored short-term gains over long-term brand health. Traditional approaches like the salesmanship model funneled most of the budget into performance campaigns, which were straightforward to measure and easy to justify.

In this scenario, marketing's influence was nebulous, its contributions to the pipeline often overshadowed by the direct and tangible results of sales efforts. The complexity of decision-making units within client organizations added layers of obscurity, as multiple stakeholders with varying priorities influenced purchasing decisions. The relationship between marketing efforts and final sales outcomes was muddled, a murky link that was difficult to elucidate with clarity and confidence.

Determined to carve out a space for marketing in a sales-dominated terrain, the CMO initiated a comprehensive market research endeavor, determined to discover a metric that could capture the true essence of their marketing efforts. Their goal was ambitious: to forge a metric that not only resonated across the boardroom but also tied neatly back to revenue, all without losing the nuance of the broader influence of marketing.

From this crucible of necessity, the concept of the "Favorable Selling Environment" (FSE) was born—a single composite metric designed to encapsulate the essence of a conducive sales atmosphere fostered by strategic marketing initiatives. FSE wasn't just another number; it was a beacon that highlighted how environmental factors, shaped by sustained brand advertising, made fertile ground for sales to flourish.

The breakthrough came when the company managed to empirically link shifts in the FSE metric to tangible impacts on revenue. This wasn't just correlation; it was causation, a clear signal through the noise proving that when FSE numbers improved, so did the company's financial outcomes. For the first time, the CMO could demonstratively show that moving the needle on FSE through thoughtful brand advertising was not just beneficial but essential.

The beauty of FSE lay in its simplicity. It was a metric that everyone, from the most hardened sales veteran to the newly minted finance analyst, could grasp and rally behind. It provided a common language, a way to articulate the previously ineffable value of marketing in a domain dominated by the direct results of sales efforts.

With FSE, marketing's role was crystallized not as a rival to sales, but as its profound enabler. It allowed for a broader, more integrated view of how market dynamics played out in the lead-up to the actual sale. No longer were marketing efforts seen as mere preliminaries to the main event of sales; they were critical, strategic maneuvers that set the stage for sales success.

The adoption of this mental model and its accompanying metric, FSE, transformed how the company perceived marketing. It fortified the

CMO's position, providing a robust shield against budget cuts and shifting the narrative from marketing as a cost center to a vital driver of corporate health. It clarified marketing's contributions in a language that resonated with every corner of the company, securing its place at the strategic heart of the organization.

## *Mental Models - An Example from the Gut*

Sometimes mental models aren't drawn up in boardrooms or pulled apart in market studies—they just spill out during a late-night call, a drink after work, or, as it happened in one noteworthy case, during an investor call by a telco CEO. It was a rare moment of clarity, unclouded by the jargon of analytics or the dizzying array of consumer data points that usually populate the industry's strategic dialogues.

"As we told you when our merger closed," the CEO said, "our plan was to expand on our fame as the industry's best value while building and becoming known for having the best network in the country. Ultimately, consumers and businesses want an available signal. And where they have available signal, they want speed and capacity, and they want that at a great price from a company that will treat them right and love them. And that's the bottom line." This wasn't just a statement; it was a revelation, an organic articulation of a mental model that was hiding in plain sight.

The model was simple yet profound, rooted deeply in the visceral needs and wants of every phone user: Fame, Value, and Love. These weren't just catchy buzzwords; they were the pillars upon which the company would rest its future strategies.

**Fame:** The company's ambition to be recognized not just as another player in the market but as a pillar of industry excellence was clear. They didn't just want to play the game; they wanted to change how the game was perceived, steering the narrative to highlight their unparalleled network quality and customer-first approach.

**Value:** In the cutthroat arena of telco giants, where every player boasts about better deals, the company aimed to redefine value. It wasn't just about competitive pricing but delivering tangible benefits that mattered—signal availability, speed, and capacity. These are the metrics that touch the daily lives of people and businesses, the very metrics that could turn a frustrated customer into a loyal advocate.

**Love:** Perhaps the most overlooked yet crucial aspect of their strategy was the promise of a relationship beyond contracts and customer service calls. This was about cultivating loyalty through genuine care, an ethos of treating customers right, and loving them in a way that transcends the usual transactional nature of business. It was a bold move to humanize the corporate giant, to make it more than a provider of services but a caretaker of its customers' needs.

The beauty of this mental model lies in its simplicity and its direct line to the core desires of consumers. It doesn't require complex diagrams or buzzwords; it's straightforward and speaks in terms that resonate both internally and externally. It paints a picture of a company not just providing a service but creating a relationship built on trust, respect, and mutual benefit.

This telco's story is a testament to the power of inherent knowledge, of leadership's ability to define and articulate a clear, compelling mental model without the crutch of external research. It's about understanding that sometimes, the most powerful tool in a marketer's arsenal is the unspoken truth that, once spoken, can define an entire strategy.

## *Fame and Flow: The New Creed of Marketing*

In a world cluttered with buzzwords and outdated paradigms, where corporations cling to simplistic models like life rafts in the digital deluge, the real essence of marketing frequently gets submerged under a sea of data and disillusion. Traditional models, like the marketing funnel or the dichotomy of Brand versus Performance, have long governed the strategic doctrines of companies large and small. These models offer the seductive simplicity of a world seen in black and white, devoid of the messy, pulsating reality of human behavior.

These classic frameworks, while neat and teachable, are crude oversimplifications that ignore the rich tapestry of consumer interactions and emotions. The funnel, for instance, presumes a linear consumer journey, a smooth slide from awareness to purchase, as if the contemporary consumer isn't bombarded at every turn by a deluge of choices and digital whispers. Similarly, the Brand vs. Performance model bifurcates the marketing world into two opposing camps, often at war over budgets and bragging rights, ignoring the symbiotic potential of holistic brand strategy.

The marketing realm cries out for a new mental model—one with the elegance to capture the latest in consumer psyche studies, yet with the clarity to be grasped by those uninitiated in the dark arts of marketing. One that doesn't just patch up the old but rethinks the very weave of marketing theory. And so, we set forth a new gospel: Fame and Flow. This isn't just another model to be tossed on the pile; it's a system for growth, a new doctrine to preach. It's a call to remember what's been forgotten: Fame is more than awareness, more than a buzzword—it's a beacon that draws consumers to brands as moths to a flame. Fame is the legend, the story, the myth that wraps around a product like a warm, inviting fog.

But Fame is nothing without its partner, Flow. Flow is the rhythm, the seamless movement from need to satisfaction. It's about crafting extraordinary, memorable interactions at every consumer touchpoint. From the first whisper of discovery to the echoes of post-purchase satisfaction, Flow is about choreographing a dance that consumers don't just passively follow but actively enjoy.

The distinction of Fame and Flow lies in its ability to merge the aspirational with the operational, the theoretical with the actionable. It respects the complexity of consumer behavior—acknowledging that customers are not mere variables in an equation to be solved but participants in a dynamic, ever-evolving relationship with brands.

In subsequent chapters, we will delve deeper into how Fame and Flow harness the latest insights from consumer psychology to mold marketing strategies that do more than drive transactions—they build energy, cultivate loyalty and propel long-term growth. We will explore case studies that illustrate how businesses have successfully implemented the Fame and Flow framework to overcome the myopic focus of outdated models and achieve sustainable market success.

### *Fame: The Neon Glow in the Market's Dark Alley*

Fame. It's a word that often makes marketers frown. It's frivolous, can't be taken seriously and surely shouldn't be discussed in boardrooms. But as we dive deep into the science of Fame, we soon realize there's much more to it; Fame is a complex construct that underpins the very essence of marketing and growth.

Scouring through the annals of marketing academia, one encounters towering figures like Byron Sharp, whose works dissect brand growth, or Professor Mark Ritson and the research duo Les Binet and Peter Field, known for their meticulous analysis of advertising effectiveness. Their research has laid down the fundamentals of what makes brands tick in the public consciousness. But our journey didn't stop at the usual suspects. We delved deeper, into the crammed shelves of System One's industry studies, through the dense prose in Paul Feldwick's writings, and into the broader, wilder world of academic pursuit that strays beyond the well-trodden path.

The realm of celebrity research provided a fresh lens through which to view brand fame. After all, the mechanisms that catapult individuals into the public eye share eerie similarities with those that propel brands into the market limelight. Academic journals and studies on societal trends offered insights into how fame works not just in marketing campaigns, but in the unpredictable, chaotic world at large.

Through this expansive research, a clearer picture of fame began to emerge, distilled into three core tenets:

**1. Exclusivity:** True to its nature, fame is not democratic. It's an elite status; a rarefied air breathed only by those who manage to rise above the noise. For brands, this means not every attempt at gaining recognition will pierce through the public's consciousness. Fame is selective, often elusive, and not easily manufactured. It's not merely about being known, but being known in a way that is markedly distinct.

**2. Longevity:** If fame were a fire, it would not burn out with the flickering of trends or the passing of a fiscal quarter. The research underscores that fame is a driver of long-term business effects. It establishes a brand so firmly in the psyche that its roots can sustain even when marketing budgets are cut, or market dynamics shift. This longevity is what separates fleeting visibility from enduring fame.

**3. Measurability:** While the ethereal quality of fame might seem beyond quantification, our research argues otherwise. There are measurable components that can gauge a brand's fame—distinctive assets, share of voice, and emotional resonance among them. These metrics provide a scaffold that can support a brand as it climbs towards higher recognition.

This foundational understanding of fame reshapes how we approach brand strategy. It's not enough to aim for short-lived spikes in recognition or to equate mere visibility with genuine fame. The goal must be to build a legacy—a brand that not only lives in the moment but endures in memory. Fame, as we've come to understand it, is not a serendipitous windfall. It's the result of deliberate, strategic craftsmanship grounded in a deep understanding of both market science and human psychology.

## *The Algebra of the Air: Calculating the Fame Quotient*

If the essence of fame could be distilled into a science, then the laboratory of the UCLA Engineering Lab circa 2013 might have come close. Their research, peculiar in its subject yet profound in its implications, delved into the annals of history, plucking World War I fighter pilots from the shadows of the past to scrutinize their fame under the harsh light of modern analytics. The query at hand was deceptively simple yet ambitiously grand: Is there a tangible link between the frequency of web mentions, Google references, and the documented achievements of these aerial combatants?

The findings? As stark as they are stirring. Fame, as it turned out, amplified not linearly, but exponentially with each victory these pilots secured. The skies of yesteryear, streaked with the trails of dogfights, told a tale of disproportionate recognition. A pilot's acclaim swelled massively with each additional notch of victory, underscoring a brutal truth about human attention: it is lavished unequally, reserved most for those who soar highest.

This phenomenon isn't confined to the war-torn skies of the early 20th century. It mirrors a broader pattern visible in every corner of human endeavor where recognition is at stake. Take, for instance, the theoretical physicist Paul Dirac, a giant in his field, yet shadowed in public memory by Einstein. Despite contributing only marginally less to the realm of physics, Dirac's fame pales exponentially compared to Einstein's. The disparity in their renown is not just a matter of academic footnotes; it is a vivid illustration of fame's exponential favoritism.

Expanding this exploration into the glitzy domain of celebrity, research from the 1990s by researcher Eric Schulman paints a similar picture. His studies sift through the stratified layers of Hollywood's glitterati, delineating a clear hierarchy of fame. 'A' list celebrities bask in the glow of public adoration, a glow ten times more intense than that enjoyed by 'B' listers, who in turn overshadow 'C' listers by another factor of ten. The pattern is relentless, a geometric progression of visibility that diminishes sharply as one moves down the tiers of stardom.

Why does this matter? In the context of marketing and branding, the implications are monumental. The dynamics of fame dictate that only a few brands, like a few illustrious pilots or iconic physicists, will capture the collective imagination in a significant way. For marketers, this reality presents a double-edged sword. On one hand, it offers a clear target—achieve breakthrough moments that catapult the brand into the higher echelons of recognition. On the other, it lays bare the immense challenge of sustaining such heightened visibility in an environment that naturally favors the few at the expense of the many.

Understanding this skewed distribution of fame is crucial for shaping effective marketing strategies. It compels brands to aim not just for incremental gains but for significant, memorable impacts that can vault them into a higher tier of consumer consciousness. This isn't about mere visibility or fleeting recognition but achieving a resonant, enduring presence that can rival the gravitational pull of the most famous names in the industry.

As marketers, we must recalibrate our expectations and strategies in light of these insights. The quest for fame in a digital age, dominated by constant information and fleeting interests, requires more than just persistence—it demands innovation, boldness, and, perhaps most importantly, an understanding of the non-linear scales at which fame operates.

## *The Numbers that Sing: The Business Ballad of Fame*

Back in 2005, the British broadcaster ITV embarked on a venture to quantify the impact of fame on business performance. Known for its massive reach, ITV wasn't just playing darts in the dark; they were meticulously scoring each throw. They introduced what they called "fame ratings," an attempt to measure the magnetic pull of their programming and its appeal to advertisers eager to piggyback on this allure.

The findings were startling in their clarity. For ITV, a mere 10% uptick in their fame rating wasn't just a notch on the belt. It translated into a staggering 20% surge in market share. Here was empirical evidence that fame wasn't just fluff. It was fuel—a potent catalyst for business growth, transforming viewer admiration into tangible market dominance.

This ITV study cracked open the door to a broader understanding, leading us straight to the seminal work of Les Binet and Peter Field. These names resonate across marketing corridors like a solemn drumbeat, heralding a deeper understanding of what drives fame. Binet and Field, through meticulous analysis, peeled back the layers on fame-driving campaigns. Their findings? Such campaigns didn't just flicker briefly in the public eye; they ignited a lasting fire.

The essence of these fame-driving efforts was twofold. First, they struck a chord, triggering an emotional resonance that went beyond the superficial. This wasn't about catching the eye; it was about clutching the heart, leaving an imprint that lingered. Second, these campaigns were inherently shareable. They sparked conversations, spread across social networks, and entrenched themselves deeply into community dialogue.

Fame, as Binet and Field articulated, was not just seen—it was felt and fervently discussed.

The metrics were unequivocal. Fame-driving campaigns dwarfed their pedestrian counterparts across a spectrum of benchmarks. Sales, profit, market penetration, loyalty, and even price sensitivity—on every front, these campaigns outshone the norms. They didn't just nudge the figures; they nudged behavior, swaying public perception and consumer actions in profound ways.

But why? Why does fame wield such power? The answer lies in its ability to elevate a brand from a mere participant in the market to a topic of cultural conversation. Fame makes a brand a protagonist in the ongoing narrative of consumers' lives, embedding it in personal and collective stories that transcend the transactional.

As marketers, these insights are not just academic; they are actionable. They compel us to reassess not just how we craft our campaigns but how we measure their success. The traditional metrics, while necessary, are insufficient alone. They need to be complemented with measures of emotional engagement and social impact—metrics that capture not just the reach but the resonance of our efforts.

In embracing this broader, more nuanced understanding of fame, we can begin to craft strategies that harness its full potential. This means creating campaigns that do more than inform—they must inspire and invigorate. It involves painting our brands not just on billboards, but into the minds and memories of our audience.

## *Defining Fame Beyond the Eyeballs*

Fame is more than visibility. It's an elusive beast, not captured by mere exposure but by a deeper, more visceral engagement. This chapter delves into the tangled underbelly of what makes something truly famous, not just known.

Fame, as it turns out, isn't just about being recognized—it's about being resonant. It's not enough for something to be visible; it must vibrate through culture, becoming a topic of conversation, a symbol of identity, or even a point of contention. The sugar on your table is ubiquitous, but it doesn't spark debates, fuel fandoms, or inspire tattoos. It's commonplace, not famous.

Fame needs a crowd, yes, but not just any crowd. It demands a choir, voices that do more than echo; they must amplify. Consider the giants that once walked the earth—Toys"R"Us, Kodak. Giants that are now whispers from the past, remembered but no longer relevant. They are recognized, but are they famous now? No, because the conversations have died, the communal fires around their brands have gone cold. Fame is not just about historical impact; it's about present relevance and ongoing dialogue.

Feldwick, that crafty cartographer of renown, lays out four corners of the fame map - Intrinsic Appeal, Mass Audiences, Distinctiveness Social Diffusion. To carve fame out of the stone of obscurity, you need all four. Like a chair with three legs, miss one, and the whole thing topples over. You need the appeal that beckons, the audience that's vast, the distinction that captivates, and the diffusion that cements it all in the social consciousness.

Byron Sharp serves it up as a dish called mental availability. It ain't just about being there; it's about being there in the mind when the wallet's out and choices loom. Sharp, with his academic rigor, talks about fame not as the flash of a neon sign but as the subtle, steady glow of a streetlamp, guiding buyers through their nocturnal purchasing journeys. This isn't about the ephemeral blaze of viral hits; it's about the constant, quiet hum of a brand in the background of everyday lives, whispering reminders through visuals and memories.

Building mental availability, as Sharp puts it, is about more than just being seen—it's about becoming a part of the consumer's mental furniture, something so familiar it's almost familial. It's about crafting those distinctive assets, those unique colors, logos, jingles, and taglines that stick in the mind like gum under a diner table. It's about ensuring that your brand isn't just in the market but in the mind, ready to be recalled at the slightest trigger of consumer desire or necessity.

Daniel Kahneman, with a Nobel Prize shining in his back pocket, paints a picture of the human mind divided, like a city at night, into two territories: System 1 and System 2. System 1 is the old neighborhood. It's intuitive, fast, and doesn't bother much with the highfalutin complexities of logic. It's where most decisions get made—in the blink of an eye, with the gut leading the way. It's the streets we walk without thinking, the turns we take without hesitating. It's where fame lives, not in the spotlight but in the shadows, in the corners of our mind we don't tidy up when company comes.

Then there's System 2, the uptown of cognition. It's analytical, deliberate, and damn slow. It's where we go when the decisions get tough, when the stakes are high and the choices aren't clear. It's the part of the mind that likes to think it's in charge, but really, it's just cleaning up after System 1's mess, rationalizing decisions already made on a deeper, darker level.

Kahneman shows us that our minds aren't the sleek, rational machines we like to think they are. They're messy, full of shortcuts and back alleys. And in this mess, fame finds its foothold. Fame, when built right, taps into System 1, embedding itself in those intuitive processes that guide most of our buying behaviors.

As marketers, understanding this dual nature of thought transforms how we approach our craft. It's not enough to appeal to the rational mind—no, we need to wedge our brands into the instinct, make them the first flicker of recognition, the first name that comes to lips, not through deliberation but through intuition.

This journey through the tangled streets of mental availability and psychological insights leaves us with a map—a way to navigate the complex interplay of awareness and subconscious recognition. It challenges us to rethink our strategies, to build campaigns that do more than inform—they must embed, resonate, and become reflex.

## *The F-Factors: Sketching the Anatomy of Fame*

So how do we define fame—our fame. Not the glossy magazine-cover version, but the kind that's ground into the pavement, that sticks to the soles of your shoes and follows you home. We're not just talking about being known; we're talking about being felt, recognized, and remembered. Fame, in our world, is the buzz in the bar after the lights come on, the graffiti that won't scrub off the wall, the tune you hum without realizing. It's widespread awareness, sure, but it's also recognition and interest that stretches from the niche to the masses, from the dedicated few to the general population.

To break down this fame into something you can work with, something you can measure and mold, we introduce the four F-Factors of Fame: Familiarity, Favorability, Feeling, and Fervor. These aren't just catchy alliterations; they are the pillars that hold up the whole rickety structure of our understanding of fame.

*Familiarity* is the first whisper of recognition. It's seeing a face in a crowded room and remembering you've seen it before. For brands, it's about known, broad "mass' awareness for most, or at minimum awareness among a clearly defined audience. It's about repeated exposure, yes, but it's more than just frequency; it's about creating a consistent, cohesive and sustained familiarity that feels ubiquitous.

*Favorability* follows Familiarity. It's not enough to be known; you have to be considered, liked, or even preferred. These are perceived differentiating qualities about the brand, product or service, whether value, quality, trust, safety, sustainability or any number of other proof points. Favorability is how we rationalize, or post-rationalize, our purchase. It's built through reinforcing positive associations, communicating benefits, testimonials, etc. And it's the rational fuel that makes people defend your brand in arguments or recommend it without hesitation.

*Feeling* dives deeper. If Favorability is a shallow nod of recognition, feeling is a deep, emotional, subconscious bond. This is System 1, mental fluency, in action. The gut reaction, the deeply rooted mental associations, instant recognition. It's the love, the passion, the rage, and the joy that your brand can inspire. It's what makes people wear your logo like a badge of honor or tattoo it on their skin. This emotional connection is what elevates a brand from a mere player in the market to a character in people's life stories.

*Fervor* is the heat that fame feeds off of. It's the intensity of the crowd at a rock concert, the chants of fans at a football game. Fervor is when interest ignites into something feverish, when passive liking turns into the talk of the town. It's when people don't just know and like your brand; they can't stop talking about it with their friends, family or coworkers around the increasingly virtual 'watercooler'.

Together, these F-Factors form a complex mosaic of what fame means in the modern marketplace. They're the colors we use to paint a picture of a brand that's not just seen but known, not just known but loved, not just loved but lived.

In the coming chapters, we'll dissect these factors further, peel back the layers, and show how they interact, how they build on one another, and how, together, they form a model of fame that's as robust as it is dynamic. This isn't just academic; it's street-smart. It's understanding fame not as a static state but as a living, breathing, evolving entity that can make or break fortunes in the flicker of an eye.

## *The Dance of Flow: Beyond the Limelight to the Checkout Line*

Fame is the spark, the siren call that brings the ships to port; but what of the harbor, the docking, the unloading of goods? That, my friends, is Flow. It's the gritty reality of the cash register, the clink of coin against coin, the swipe of credit on terminal. It's one thing to fill the air with your tune, but another to dance to it.

Flow, in its essence, is about smoothing the path from desire to fulfillment. It's the grease on the gears, the oil in the engine, the ease of the journey from "I want this" to "I have this." And it's not just about that first purchase. No, it's about the second, the third, about turning fleeting fancies into lasting loyalties.

Flow is the quiet powerhouse, often overshadowed by the bluster of Fame but no less critical. You see, Les Binet and Peter Field's research confirms that growth doesn't come from fame or flow alone. It comes from their confluence, from the harmonious blend of long-term brand building and short-term sales activation. They argue, and we agree, that even the most ambitious fame-driving campaigns must incorporate mechanisms not just to swell the tide of demand but to harness it, channel it, convert it into sales.

So, what does Flow look like in practice? It's the seamless checkout process on a website that remembers your preferences and predicts your needs. It's the customer service that doesn't just solve your problem but anticipates it. It's the offer that arrives not just at the right place but precisely at the right moment. It's about creating experiences so fluid, so frictionless, that the customer barely notices the passage from interest to ownership.

This isn't just theory. It's knowing that every touchpoint, every interaction with your customer, is an opportunity to either enhance the Flow or to dam it. Every hiccup in the process, every moment of friction, is a leak in your pipeline, a crack in your foundation.

But let's take it further, because it's not enough to understand flow in isolation. Just as a river flows fastest at its bends, flow in marketing accelerates when it curves around the contours of fame. The campaigns that truly convert, that truly drive growth, are those that weave these elements together. They build on the brand's fame to create pathways that are not just easy but inevitable for the customer to follow.

So, as we pull the truth about marketing into focus, remember this: Fame sets the stage, but flow steals the show. It's the quiet operator behind the scenes, turning the bright lights of fame into the hard cash of business success. And as we delve deeper into the mechanisms of flow in the next chapters, keep your eyes on the prize: a system where fame and flow work not just in tandem but as two parts of a greater whole, driving growth that's as sustainable as it is spectacular.

*Navigating the Currents of Flow: The Tangibility of Availability*

The concept of flow in marketing isn't just about smooth operations or sexy interfaces; it's about presence, both physical and digital. It's about ensuring that when the moment of decision comes, your brand isn't just an option; it's the inevitable choice. For a brand to ingrain itself into the daily lives of consumers, it must be physically available, captivating in its messaging, and seamless in experience.

Byron Sharp lays it out clearly in his gospel of growth. He preaches the doctrine of mental availability to build fame, sure, but he pairs it with the creed of physical availability. In his view, the easier a brand is to notice and buy, the more it grows. He cites a study from '95, found tucked away in his seminal book, illustrating an exponential relationship between physical availability and market share. The logic is brutally simple: more visibility leads to more sales leads to more shelf space—a virtuous cycle where market share feeds on itself.

Yet, physical availability isn't just about dominating shelf space in brick-and-mortar retail. No, this battleground has digital fronts too. We used to marvel at Walmart's endless aisles, but today we scroll through Amazon's digital shelves, where visibility is measured not in feet but in fractions of a scroll. Tomorrow, we'll navigate the even narrower corridors of AI-driven platforms, where algorithms decide which single product best fits your needs before you even know you need it.

*Sharp distills the essence of physical availability into three potent elements.*

*Presence:* your brand must be easily accessible across a broad range of purchasing scenarios. Whether it's a midnight craving or a noonday impulse, your product should be there, waiting to be picked up.

*Prominence:* in a world where every shelf screams for attention, your brand needs to shout louder. It's not just about being there; it's about standing out. When a consumer's finger hovers over a screen or their eyes scan a shelf, your brand should cut through the noise, making competitors fade into the background.

*Relevance:* your timing and context must align with consumer needs. Selling sunscreen in December might work in Australia but flops in Alaska. Your product might be noticeable and easy to buy, but if it's not pertinent to the consumer's current context, it's just another pretty face in the crowd.

As we delve deeper into the mechanics of flow, we confront a marketplace that's increasingly fragmented, where digital and physical realms collide and merge. The challenge is no longer just to be present but to dominate the consumer's limited attention span across all fronts.

## *The Precision of Persuasion: Timing & Message in the Dance of Desire*

In 2020, Google rolled out a sly experiment, a cunning play in the game of brand switching. They snagged customers on the brink of a shopping spree and asked them about their first-choice brand. Then, they targeted ads at these shoppers, peddling entirely fictional brands crafted from the clay of behavioral science. The results? A disturbingly effective demonstration of allegiance swapping, all thanks to some well-timed words.

But there was more to it. The effectiveness of this tactic swung wildly across product categories. Take cereal, for example. Only about 28% of shoppers were swayed to ditch their go-to brand. It seems that our morning rituals are coated with a thick layer of loyalty, resistant to even the slickest of advertising maneuvers. On the other hand, for products tethered more to rational favorability hooks like cost or convenience—think hotels and car insurance—up to 80% of consumers were persuaded to jump ship.

From this deep dive into the psyche of the shopper, Google distilled a trio of lessons on maximizing flow:

**1. Constant Presence:** Byron Sharp wasn't joking when he preached the gospel of presence. From the very spark of a consumer's interest, your brand needs to be there, findable, looming large over the competition. Miss that initial moment, and you might just miss the boat entirely.

**2. Streamlined Pathways:** The purchase funnel should be a slipstream, not a slog. The longer your potential buyers linger within it, the greater the chance they'll be seduced by the siren songs of competitors.

Trim the fat from the buying process; make it as direct and undemanding as possible.

**3. Timely and Tuned-in Messages:** If the right message at the right time can steer a customer away from their favorite cereal, imagine what it can do in less sentimentally charged categories. It's about locking into the consumer's current mental state, their immediate needs and wants, and hitting them with a message that resonates so deeply it feels like fate.

This tactic of hyper-relevant messaging isn't just a neat trick—it's what customers have come to expect. The era of broad-spectrum advertising is fading into the smog. Today, retargeted ads boast higher click-through rates, higher engagement, and higher conversion rates. People don't just tolerate personalized ads; they prefer them. They crave interactions that acknowledge their past behaviors, that speak directly to their swirling desires and immediate needs. Marketers just need to toe the fine line between personal and creepy.

## *The F-Factors: Defining the Currents of Flow*

Flow—this isn't just a river of revenue, it's a relentless current that pulls customers along a journey marked by engagement and ease. So, what really stitches up this seamless tapestry of interactions that we call customer Flow? Well, it's built on a bedrock of experiences that aren't just enjoyable but downright necessary if you want to keep your customers from jumping ship.

Here are the four F-Factors that build Flow, each one a critical cog in the machine that drives customer retention and satisfaction.

**1. Findability:** This is your beacon in the fog, the lighthouse that guides the weary consumer to your shores. It's about making sure your brand pops up exactly when and where it should. Visibility isn't just about being seen; it's about being found at that critical moment of need.

**2. Facilitation:** Here's where things get slick. Facilitation is the grease on the wheels of the customer journey. It's about smoothing out any bumps that might snag the purchasing process or snag it again when they come back for more. This is the art of making the next step—whether it's buying or rebuying—seem as natural as drawing a breath.

**3. Fascination:** This isn't just about catching the eye; it's about capturing the heart and mind. Fascination is measured by how your content performs, how it engages. It's about delivering that killer message at just the right time to make the consumer think, "Hell, yes!" and take action.

**4. Following:** The final frontier of Flow is about building lasting bonds. It's not just about making a sale; it's about nurturing a relationship that keeps them coming back and actively recommending or advocating on the brand's behalf. Following is fostered through direct, first-party interactions that deepen engagement and foster loyalty.

These four F-Factors of Flow are not just theoretical constructs; they are practical tools, measurable and manageable, that can significantly boost how effectively a brand engages with its market.

Now, let's dive deeper into the mechanics and the magic of these eight F-Factors—four powering Fame and four driving Flow. Each factor is a chapter of its own, each story a lesson in leveraging what we know to amplify what we can achieve. We will unpack each factor with realism and raw data. We'll provide backstory, bring in case studies, and show where the real opportunities lie to drive business growth.

# CHAPTER 3

## DISSECTING FAME & FLOW

### *Familiarity: The Foundation of Fame*

In the trenches of the marketing battlefield, familiarity is not just a buzzword—it's the artillery that blasts open the doors to consumers' minds. It's about how deeply a brand or product is ingrained in the public consciousness. Awareness, in its rawest form, isn't just about knowing; it's about being the first that comes to mind, the default, the reflex. And in the high stakes game of market share, the more familiar your brand, the bigger slice of the pie you command.

This chapter dives into Familiarity, peeling back its layers to reveal how it's constructed and how it can be manipulated to serve broader strategic ambitions.

Take the case of Overstock in the U.S. Once a marketplace for surplus goods, Overstock faced a branding crisis; it was perceived as a last resort for stuff others didn't want, not a first choice. The solution? They seized an opportunity that was nothing short of audacious. As Bed Bath & Beyond, a big box retailer known for its namesake goods, spiraled into bankruptcy, Overstock did the unthinkable: they bought the rights to the Bed Bath & Beyond name, effectively hijacking decades of built-up brand familiarity. Overnight, Overstock wasn't just a surplus goods outlet anymore; it was a household name. By co-opting the Familiarity that Bed Bath & Beyond had cultivated, Overstock rebooted its brand identity, leveraging the existing mental real estate that the name occupied in consumers' minds.

But how we build this Familiarity is evolving, fragmenting into a mosaic of media strategies that challenge the traditional. It's no longer just the heavy artillery of TV ads driving the charge. With global TV ad revenues on the decline, the landscape demands innovation, a guerrilla approach to capturing consumer attention.

Consider the ingenious campaign by Radio France. Tasked with engaging a younger audience with classical music, a genre typically reserved for older demographics, they took a path less traveled. They partnered with Tinder, the modern-day cupid's playground, to create profiles for composers like Tchaikovsky and Mozart, but with a twist. These weren't just profiles; they were gateways into the world of classical music, dressed up in contemporary culture and interactive fun. This wasn't just marketing; it was matchmaking, introducing young listeners to classical music through a medium they understood and appreciated.

This strategy embodies the essence of modern familiarity-building: it's daring, it's unconventional, and it taps into the zeitgeist of its audience. It's about meeting your audience where they are, not where you wish they'd be.

As marketers, the challenge is to adapt and thrive in this fractured media world. The question we must constantly ask ourselves is stark: how do we maximize our reach where our customers are already engaged? Whether they're swiping on Tinder, scrolling through Instagram, or binge-watching YouTube, each platform offers a unique doorway to brand familiarity.

The old playbook—dominated by TV spots and print ads—is being rewritten in real time. Today's marketing requires a blend of boldness and creativity, using every tool in the digital arsenal to embed our brands in the daily lives of our consumers.

### Initiative Case Study on Supercharging Familiarity, Fast:
*Amazon Prime Video's Fallout*

In April 2024, Amazon Prime Video was rolling the dice hard, betting big on a show born from the cult fervor of gamers—Fallout, set in a post-apocalyptic wasteland. The goal was clear: turn Fallout into an event, the kind that etches itself into the minds of the masses, making it the talk of every town, not just among those that spend their evenings in role-playing video games.

With the sands of time slipping fast from trailer drop to premiere night, in barely two weeks, Amazon Prime Video unfurled a campaign of mass seduction. This was about more than just catching eyes; it was about capturing imaginations, creating a buzz so loud it couldn't be ignored. The streaming giant wasn't playing small; they deployed an arsenal of media tactics designed to blitz the senses and sear the show into public consciousness.

The strategy was a spectacle of modern "Familiarity" marketing. Iconography from Fallout—the stark, haunting visuals of a nuclear wasteland—became the bat signal for fans and newcomers alike. At the core of the campaign was the raw, unfiltered presentation of the post-apocalyptic saga, mirroring the mundane struggles and survivalist ethos of its characters. Instead of glossy, airbrushed billboards, streets were plastered with weathered, graffiti-tagged posters. Animatronic billboards didn't just show ads; they played out scenes, creating a mini-theatrical experience for every passerby. Public transit wasn't just a way to get from point A to B; it was a journey through the Fallout wasteland, with each subway car and bus stop transformed into scenes from the game-turned-show. This wasn't just advertising; it was a brutal invasion of the public space, where the decay of the billboards mirrored the decay of the Fallout world.

The show took over Twitch, turning gameplay into watch parties where the lines between game and show blurred into one continuous digital experience. Every stream was an invitation, every click a potential convert. This wasn't just advertising; it was immersion. To send shockwaves through key communities, AR recreations of Fallout icons like the Pip-Boy and Power Suit breached gaming spaces; serving as a bat signal to fans. A Fallout-themed Twitch livestream immersed viewers in its world with vault-dweller costumes and apocalyptic-but-fun design. Dynamic HPTOs cornered Reddit and IGN to build buzz, and allowed intrigued gamers and eager TV fans to announce their excitement by donning a Power Armor suit via a custom Snap lens. There was something on the menu for those less apt to Snap, a partnership with "apocalypse optimist" comedian Max Fosh, serving Fallout's favorite food – bugs - to unsuspecting food critics, enticing entertainment lovers.

In this campaign, nothing was sleek; everything bore the marks of a lived-in, rugged world. The effect was magnetic. And the numbers rolled in: 45 million trailer views before the sun rose on opening night. In the two weeks following the premiere, 65 million viewers—hooked, obsessed. Fallout wasn't just Amazon's big bet anymore; it was the biggest, most successful show ever on the platform, outshining even the mega-budget anthology The Lord of the Rings: Rings of Power.

The collateral effects were staggering: a 7,500% spike in game sales, echoing the show's magnetic pull. In the world of the streaming wars, where viewers are besieged by endless choices, Fallout carved out its dominion—not just through visibility but through a visceral, unignorable presence. It was a masterclass in using media not just to inform or entertain, but to envelop and dominate, transforming Fallout into a synonym for innovation in adaptation and a textbook case for mass familiarity in the digital age.

**How to Build Familiarity**

So how do you etch your brand into the minds of the masses when they're bombarded by a relentless stream of information from all corners? Here's how to cut through the noise and expand your brand's horizon to the furthest reaches of the market.

*Step 1: Define Your Battlefield*

You can't shoot in the dark and expect to hit the target. Define who you're trying to reach. This isn't about throwing a wide net and hoping for the best. It's about understanding exactly who needs to hear your message. Age, interests, habits, where they hang out online and offline. The more precise you are, the better you can tailor your strategies to be where they are, not where you hope they'd be.

*Step 2: Craft a Message That Sticks*

Your message needs to stick. It's got to resonate, reverberate, and remain. What's the core thing you want them to remember? Strip down your message to its bare bones—make it simple, memorable, and sharp as a tack. This message is your war cry, your anthem, the chant that will echo through the virtual and physical streets.

*Step 3: Consider Every Megaphone*

The media landscape isn't just fragmented; it's shattered. To build mass awareness, you need to pick up every piece and make it sing for you. Think of every channel possible—social media, TV, radio, outdoor, digital banners, podcasts, and hell, even the odd bathroom stall if that's what it takes. Then prioritize your channels through mix modeling or just use your gut. Multi-channel assaults make your brand unavoidable.

*Step 4: Make Allies, Not Ads*

Influence travels faster through networks of trust. Partner with influencers, brand ambassadors, and even other brands. Let them carry your message into their circles of influence. These partnerships should feel organic, not forced—more like comrades in arms than paid mercenaries. Their authenticity will be the Trojan horse that carries your message past consumer defenses.

*Step 5: Turn Volume Into Strategy*

When it comes to awareness, volume matters. This isn't the time for subtlety; it's the time for saturation. Plan your media spends and content drops to create bursts of overwhelming presence. Think of it as a bass drum of brand exposure—short, sharp shocks designed to imprint your brand on the collective consciousness. And maintain exposure by managing your reach and frequency.

Building familiarity in today's fragmented media landscape is like trying to conduct an orchestra in the middle of a rock concert. It's messy, it's loud, and it's chaotic, but with the right strategy, your brand can be the melody that cuts through the madness.

## *Favorability: The Delicate Dance of Likability & Preference*

Favorability is not just about being liked; it's about being preferred, about building a connection so strong that your brand becomes the default choice even before the wallet is out. It is the quiet magic of emotional bonds and the sharp science of distinct advantages. It's what makes a brand not only visible but viable, not just known but needed. This duality of likability and preference is the twin engine that drives a brand up the ladder of consumer choice. Think about how you shop for a winter coat. Before you even hit the stores or start scrolling online, you've likely got a couple of brands dancing in your head. That's Favorability at play—your brain's guest list for the shopping spree.

But there's another side to Favorability, beyond just being liked. It's about preference, about carving out a distinct position that cuts through the market noise to highlight what makes your brand or product different—and better. It's about that coat that doesn't just keep you warm but promises to be the bulwark against the worst sub-zero days. That's Favorability doing its job, making you not just a choice, but the choice.

Consider the often-overlooked egg aisle. Here's a place where brand recognition is as thin as the shells on the shelf. For most, brands in the egg category don't ring any bells. You face a sea of options: organic, pasture-raised, omega-enriched. Each carton squawks a different call, but it's all white noise. Here, Favorability is the beacon that can guide bewildered consumers through the fog.

Enter the Honest Eggs Company from Australia—a brand that cracked the Favorability code in an unexpectedly brilliant way. Knowing that their market was cluttered and every brand signaled an ethical and sustainable choice, they needed a standout strategy. Their masterstroke? They put step counters on their chickens and showcased these stats directly on the eggs themselves. It was a simple, clear message: our eggs come from chickens that actually walk, as demonstrated by the FitChix tracker, not just flap around in a cramped cage. They didn't stop there—they made waves with out-of-home advertising, a cheeky video, and even created a Strava account for a chicken, blending humor with transparency.

But the real genius was in making the campaign visible right where it counts: on the product itself, right at that critical moment of decision in the grocery aisle. This wasn't just advertising; it was smart communication, ensuring that when consumers reached for a carton, they weren't just picking up eggs—they were making a choice they felt good about. Honest Eggs knew what mattered to their customers and presented it in the clearest way possible.

This strategy highlights a critical aspect of building Favorability: understanding what your customers value and how you can distinctly and effectively communicate that your product meets those needs better than others. In a world where every brand vies for attention, Favorability is about ensuring your message isn't just seen but felt, turning passive viewers into passionate buyers.

So, as you ponder how to elevate your brand, consider this: Favorability isn't about being the loudest in the room; it's about being the voice that speaks directly to the heart of consumer desires. It's about finding that unique attribute, that special something that makes your product not just a part of the conversation but the focal point.

**Initiative Case Study:**
*How To Move An Entire Country To Favor Rexona*

In the depths of Buenos Aires, where city blocks are cluttered with cafes and street vendors peddling yesterday's dreams, the specter of sedentarism stalks the bustling streets. Argentina, draped in the vibrant rhythms of tango and the frenetic pace of urban life, harbors a silent killer — physical inactivity. The World Health Organization has placed the nation among the top five most sedentary countries globally, a statistic that grew only more alarming with the Covid pandemic's lingering shadow.

Rexona, the leading deodorant brand (also known as Degree in other parts of the world), faced its own battle amidst this inertia. Found in four out of ten homes across Argentina, its market penetration had seen a worrying decline, dropping almost three points since December '21. The connection was painfully clear: no sweat, no need for deodorant. Rexona's business, thriving on the sweat of a moving nation, found itself gasping for air in an increasingly static society.

In a bold move against this tide, Rexona launched "Primeros Pasos" (First Steps), an initiative that aimed to disrupt the sedentary cycle by confronting the very fears that anchored its populace to inactivity. The campaign didn't sugarcoat the challenges; it exposed the grim reality of a society trapped by its own excuses—"Tomorrow, I will start exercising"— a tomorrow that, for many, never dawned.

The campaign unfolded in a gritty narrative that cut through the glossy veneers of traditional personal care advertising – a hero video aired across social media and cinema screens, laying bare the raw data of sedentarism's toll on the Argentine populace. The video transitioned into stories of ordinary Argentines, not sculpted athletes or fitness "influencers", but everyday people grappling with the inertia of their lives.

The brand mobilized consumers through a digital platform, launched through QR codes on product packaging, a portal to their first exercise class for free. This wasn't just about moving bodies; it was about shifting mindsets. In gyms and sports centers across the country, first-timers, surrounded by peers equally unversed in the art of exercise, took tentative steps towards a more active life. Rexona partnered with over fifteen institutions across more than fourteen activities, ensuring that no potential mover felt left behind.

The results spoke volumes. Over 150,000 Argentines attended their first free class, with a staggering 87% continuing regularly. Primeros Pasos drove significant improvement in Rexona's Favorability (+13ppt YoY) and Purchase Intent (+14ppt YoY) leading to +6 points in Penetration versus the prior year - reaching number one among women for the first time and maintaining its leadership among men.

In the narrative of "Primeros Pasos," Rexona rewrote the story of a sedentary nation, turning silent streets into stages of sweat and perseverance. The campaign, raw and unfiltered, didn't just sell deodorant—it sold a new way of life, one where every step, however small, was a victory against the creeping death of inactivity.

### How to Build Favorability

Favorability isn't about slapping a smile on your product and hoping people love it because it grins back. No, it's about getting under their skin, in the good way, making them prefer your product as if it's the last drink in a desert bar. Here's how you do it, step by step.

### Step 1: Understand Their Love Language

First off, know what your customers cherish. This isn't about what you think they should value, but what they actually do. Conduct surveys, delve into social media conversations, or engage directly through community forums. Find out their pain points, desires, and what makes them tick. This understanding is the bedrock of favorability.

### Step 2: Spotlight Your Unique Selling Proposition (USP)

Your product needs a hook, something that not only catches their eye but keeps them coming back. This could be your groundbreaking technology, an unheard-of warranty, or customer service that makes them feel like the CEO. Whatever it is, make sure it's something your competitors can't or don't offer. Your USP should scream from rooftops, "I'm what you need, and here's why."

### Step 3: Quality Isn't a Luxury; It's a Necessity

Nothing kills favorability like a product that talks big but walks small. Ensure your product not only meets but exceeds industry standards. Quality assurance should be your watchword. A good product gets tried; a great one gets bought again. And in the world of reviews and social proof, quality can echo much louder and longer than any marketing campaign.

### Step 4: Tell Your Story

Every product has a story, and if yours doesn't, you better start writing it fast. People cling to narratives much stronger than they do to features.

Your product's backstory—why it exists, the problems it solves, and the dreams it fulfills—can convert your audience's mild interest into a strong preference. Use your platforms to tell this story consistently, be it through blogs, videos, or podcasts.

*Step 5: Demonstrate Value in Their Real World*

Show, don't just tell. Use case studies, testimonials, and real-life examples of how your product lives in the world. Make the benefits tangible. When people see others like them benefiting from your product, the mental barriers to trying it lower. They don't just see a product; they see a solution to a familiar problem.

Building favorability for your product is like nurturing a rough diamond. It's not just about the intrinsic quality of the stone but about the craft and care that transforms it into a gem they desire. Walk these steps like you mean it and watch as favorability for your product grows from the roots of genuine customer satisfaction and real-world effectiveness.

## *Feeling & the Power of Distinctive Media Assets*

Let's break down Feeling, the gut response your brand evokes. It's about those invisible threads—mental availability and System 1 thinking—that tie a consumer to a brand without them even knowing why they feel that pull. This isn't just about knowing your brand exists; it's about making your brand the first that springs to mind, the one that feels like an old friend in the chaos of choice.

Here's where the essence of a brand comes into play—its soul, if you will. The mascots, jingles, taglines, the colors and shapes that splash across the subconscious before you even realize you're remembering them. It's the McDonald's arches, the Nike swoosh, the quick, comforting ping of an iPhone text. These aren't just marketing tools; they're the hooks that embed your brand in the public psyche, making it instantly recognizable, making it feel like home.

This feeling, it's not accidental. It's the result of meticulous crafting and endless repetition, a consistency that brands must maintain to ensure these symbols and sounds don't just pass through the mind like so much static. But it's a fine line. Change too much, too fast, and you risk severing the ties that bind your customers to you.

Take the debacle with Twitter and its rebrand to 'X'. It was akin to Coca-Cola ditching its iconic bottle but keeping the drink the same. Overnight, a symbol that had become synonymous with real-time conversation, with the very idea of 'tweeting', was gone. What followed was a disorienting void for users who suddenly found a piece of their digital vernacular missing, a shared identity obscured. This wasn't just a rebrand; it was a cultural erasure, a misstep that cost dearly in terms of brand equity.

But Feeling isn't just crafted in the creative departments. Media, too, plays its pivotal role. Media properties themselves can become distinctive assets. Consider the Michelin Guide, originally crafted to encourage car travel, and thus tire usage. Today, it's the gold standard in dining, a far cry from its utilitarian origins but an indelible part of the Michelin brand story. Such media moves transcend traditional advertising, offering utility, identity, and prestige—all elements that enhance mental availability.

What could be your version of the Michelin Guide? What unique assets do you already possess that could be transformed into distinctive media properties? How do you ensure that your media not only reaches but resonates, building those crucial mental structures that enhance both immediate recognition and enduring loyalty?

As you reflect on these questions, consider the broader implications for your media strategy. It's about transforming every point of contact into a moment of connection, turning every exposure into an opportunity to deepen the brand experience, to embed your brand not just in the market, but in the minds and hearts of your audience.

✤ ◆ ✤ ◆ ✤ ◆ ✤ ◆

**Dove & Initiative Case Study on Cultivating Feeling:**
*Casting Beleza Real*

Dove has long positioned itself as a vanguard in the battle against the beauty industry's often narrow standards. With its "Real Beauty" campaign, Dove has not only challenged these norms but has become one of the most recognizable brands in its category. This case study delves into how Dove refreshed its enduring message in Portugal, continuously cultivating its strong association with Real Beauty among young women challenged by the pressures of social media.

The advent of social media has ushered in a not-so-subtle revolution in how beauty is perceived, especially among young women in Portugal. Recent studies indicated a crisis of confidence, with a staggering 76% of young females reluctant to post a photo online without the digital veil of a filter. Dove saw an urgent need to alter this narrative and reinforce its brand ethos to a new generation and their families.

The insight was piercing in its clarity: Mainstream media, rather than alleviating these pressures, was compounding them. Glossy, unrealistic portrayals of beauty dominated every screen, embedding unhealthy standards into the daily lives of millions.

Dove's strategy pivoted on redefining mainstream beauty narratives. The plan was to transcend mere discussions about real beauty to showcasing it on a grand stage, making real beauty and self-esteem central themes in popular culture. This strategy was aimed at nurturing a profound brand feeling, transforming Dove from a mere participant in the beauty conversation to a principal conductor.

Dove initiated a partnership with SIC, Portugal's premier soap opera channel, embedding its campaign within the popular "Sangue Oculto" soap opera. This program was chosen for its wide reach and its emotional grip on viewers. In a bold move, Dove conducted open auditions for real girls to star in the soap opera, eschewing professional actresses. This not only democratized the process but also ensured that the campaign's protagonists were relatable figures, embodying the very real beauty Dove aimed to spotlight.

The selected participants were written into the existing narrative of "Sangue Oculto," engaging in 32 scenes that tackled the pervasive issue of social media's impact on self-esteem. These scenes were crafted to resonate emotionally, portraying struggles and triumphs that viewers could empathize with and learn from.

The entire journey, from auditions to episodic developments, was chronicled across Dove's paid, earned, and owned channels. This holistic approach turned the campaign into a living, breathing dialogue with the audience, at a massive scale.

The impact of the "Casting Beleza Real" campaign was profound. The campaign reached an estimated 4 million people, about 40% of the Portuguese population. It sparked widespread conversation, significantly on social platforms, where discussions about real beauty and self-esteem flourished. The mental association (Feeling) of Dove's Real Beauty message strengthened by +25%. The campaign translated into measurable sales growth, both in volume and value, underscoring the efficacy of emotional connections in driving business performance.

The "Casting Beleza Real" initiative went beyond mere advertising; it was a cultural intervention that repositioned Dove at the heart of the real beauty discourse. By integrating real-life stories and real people into mainstream media, Dove not only changed how beauty is portrayed but how it is perceived and discussed in everyday life.

Dove's campaign in Portugal exemplifies how brands can effectively generate profound feeling through strategic media partnerships and content integration. By aligning its campaign with genuine social concerns and leveraging popular culture, Dove strengthened its brand fame, ensuring that its message of real beauty resonated deeply, widely, and enduringly. This case study underscores the power of emotion in marketing and its critical role in driving fame and business success. Through thoughtful, resonant campaigns, brands can turn societal challenges into powerful narratives that not only support commercial objectives but also contribute positively to social discourse.

✦ ✦ ✦ ✦ ✦ ✦ ✦ ✦

### Initiative Case Study on How Emotional Connection Scored a Brand Win for Feeling:
*NRMA Insurance Cricket Covers*

The strategic creation of distinctive media assets isn't confined to century-old tire companies. Modern brands can also cultivate their own unique media landscapes. A notable example comes from Australia, where NRMA Insurance leveraged the nation's love for cricket by associating itself with cricket covers.

Cricket, more than just a sport in Australia, is a seasonal celebration that commands attention across the nation. NRMA Insurance, stepping into a long legacy of previous sponsorships, faced the challenge of redefining its association with cricket to reflect its brand message of being "Australia's most helpful insurer." The task was monumental: replace over two decades of ingrained sponsor associations and carve out a significant presence in a fiercely competitive arena. NRMA Insurance has a unique opportunity to leverage Australia's cultural passion for cricket to foster deep emotional engagement and enhance mental availability.

The strategic team dove deep into the annals of cricket history, unearthing a quirky yet frequent disruption in Sydney's cricket matches: rain delays. Sydney, notorious for its wet weather during the cricket season, presented a unique media opportunity—cricket covers. This insight was the key to transforming NRMA Insurance's sponsorship into a distinctive asset that drives mental availability.

NRMA Insurance turned wet-weather cricket covers into canvases for storytelling. The idea was to convert these covers into symbols of NRMA Insurance's commitment to help, ensuring that even rain delays could be turned into opportunities for brand visibility and engagement. The covers featured prominently in broadcasts, providing over 6.5 hours of main broadcast exposure at no additional cost.

The NRMA Insurance Cricket Covers campaign not only achieved but exceeded its objectives, demonstrating the power of Feeling. By creating mental availability through emotional connections and distinctive assets, the campaign achieved over 6.5 hours of broadcast coverage, equating to an estimated media value of over $3.36 million. It garnered 50 pieces of editorial content worth over $650,000. Association with "helpfulness" increased by 5%, exceeding the target by 1.5 times. Website traffic also increased 10% doubling the campaign goal. But above all, NRMA Insurance quickly became one of the most recognized cricket sponsors, a significant feat against competitors with decades of sponsorship history.

**How to Build Feeling**

Carving out a distinct emotional connection with your consumers is the equivalent of a secret handshake. It's subtle, it's powerful, and it's effective. Let's strip it down to the basics and talk about building that elusive feeling for your brand.

*Step 1: Pin Down the Emotional Core*

First things first, identify the core emotion your brand stands for. Is it security, joy, nostalgia, rebellion? This isn't about what your product does, but how it makes people feel. You're not selling beer; you're selling camaraderie. You're not peddling insurance; you're providing peace of mind. Find that emotional core and everything you do should emanate from this epicenter.

*Step 2: Consistency is Your Best Friend*

Once you've latched onto your core emotion, consistency becomes your most loyal ally. From your visuals and messaging to your customer service and product experience—everything should reinforce this feeling. Consistent positive experiences lead to memorable emotional imprints. Let every interaction leave a trace of the feeling you want to evoke.

*Step 3: Tell a Story, Don't State Facts*

People remember stories, not data. Weave your brand's core emotion into narratives that stick. Use stories that reflect common customer experiences, aspirational journeys, or even cautionary tales—all dripping with your brand's essence. This is practical storytelling: not just who your brand is, but how it fits into the real lives of your consumers.

### Step 4: Engage the Senses

A multi-sensory approach embeds deeper emotional connections. If your brand were a concert, what would it sound like? If it were a meal, what would it taste like? Sharp's principles remind us that distinctive brand assets trigger recognition—so think beyond visuals. Consider sounds, smells, and textures that can be associated with your brand. This sensory branding doesn't just build recognition; it cements emotional bonds.

### Step 5: Humanize Your Brand

Brands that feel like old friends stand the test of time. Show your brand's human side. Share your triumphs and your failures. Engage in real conversations with your customers. Use platforms that allow for two-way interactions—social media, customer service platforms, even old-fashioned phone calls. Let your audience see the people behind the products.

Building a feeling for your brand isn't about manipulating emotions; it's about connecting on a human level. It's about making your brand a reliable presence that aligns with the values and desires of your audience. Do this right, and you won't just have customers—you'll have brand advocates who feel deeply connected to your narrative and your success.

## *Fervor: The Wildfire of Word-of-Mouth*

In this exploration into the dynamics of brand growth, we now reach the pulsating heart of social transmission: Fervor. This isn't just about people knowing your brand; it's about them talking about it, spreading it like wildfire across social platforms and beyond. Here, marketing transcends the transactional and becomes a cultural phenomenon.

Jonah Berger, author of *Contagious*, argues compellingly that while ads play their part, nothing boosts a brand like the buzz of the crowd. Word of mouth, he insists, wields a power that is not just equal to traditional advertising but surpasses it tenfold. It's the endorsement no money can buy—the nod from one person to another that says, "This is worth your time."

Take the curious case of Maison Margiela's Tabi shoes. In the fall of 2023, a storm brewed not from celebrity endorsements or pricey ad campaigns but from a viral moment born on TikTok. Alexis DuJay aired her grievance over a stolen pair of $800 Tabis, and suddenly, these cult-status shoes were catapulted from niche to mainstream, with Google searches surging by 347% and sellouts spiking by 36%. This wasn't planned; it was spontaneous combustion in the digital age, turning obscurity into ubiquity overnight.

Nike's Colin Kaepernick ad campaign was different; it was a calculated gamble that blazed across social channels and media outlets. Opening with a seemingly effortlessly simple, understated tweet of Kaepernick's face and the words, "Believe in something. Even if it means sacrificing everything," Nike did more than sell shoes—they sold a stance, a worldview, turning their brand into a banner for social justice and personal conviction. This wasn't quiet strategy; it was loud, disruptive, impossible to ignore. The campaign ignited fierce debates, boycott threats, and undying support, amplifying Nike's presence in the cultural conversation exponentially. This wasn't just creating buzz; it was stoking a wildfire, watching the sparks catch, and leaving the world to deal with the blaze—a master class in planning for fervor.

These stories exemplify the dual nature of Fervor: sometimes a wild, untamable beast that breaks free without warning, and at other times, a creature meticulously bred for spectacle and impact. Both scenarios underscore a crucial truth: Fervor thrives on connection—between people, between stories, and between the brand and its audience.

✧ ◆ ✧ ◆ ✧ ◆ ✧ ◆

### Initiative Case Study in Fervor Put to Work:
*The LEGO Piece Garden*

In a bold move, The LEGO Group launched the "The LEGO Piece Garden" campaign, transforming a corner of the London Design Festival into a sprawling, interactive LEGO garden. This wasn't just any garden; it was a monument to the imaginative power lying dormant in every adult, waiting to be unleashed through the simple snap of a LEGO piece.

"The LEGO Piece Garden" was no small endeavor. Working with It's Nice That, the partnership came to life as a vibrant, living sculpture. Sprawling over 200 square meters, and featuring over a million individual LEGO pieces, this ten-day immersive exhibition was programmed with hands-on build experiences, photo moments and artist workshops.

Attendees were not just observers; they were participants, invited contribute their own floral creations built with LEGO bricks to the installation, reflecting their personal creativity and flair. Growing in the space over time, each addition told a story. From the LEGOburnam (a flower which sprouts whenever someone has a good idea), to the Cringing Lily (a flower which reminds you of your teenage bedroom), each brick-made bloom was a testament to the unleashed creativity of an adult rediscovering play.

With a limited budget, the campaign couldn't rely on massive ad buys or traditional media channels. Instead, The LEGO Group turned to guerrilla marketing tactics and targeted social media to spark the flame of fervor. Pop-up LEGO gardens appeared overnight in unexpected corners of London—from busy Tube stations to popular public squares—each installation inviting passersby to transform their morning commute with a touch of creativity.

Influencers and creators were enlisted to showcase their own LEGO creations on social media, blending LEGO bricks into high art and everyday objects, thus blurring the lines between play and professional practice. Influential artists-in-residence, Charlotte Mei and Alec Doherty, were tasked with building original work using LEGO Art sets throughout the activation and hosted hands-on workshops within The LEGO Piece Garden space, guiding attendees on how to use LEGO bricks as a medium for expression and artistry.

The results were staggering. Over 50,000 participants interacted with The LEGO Piece Garden during the festival. Social media fervor skyrocketed by 250%, with viral videos showing time-lapse creations and testimonials from participants. The LEGO Piece Garden generated over

15x pieces of National Press coverage, including in *The Times* and Metro. Post-campaign surveys indicated a 60% increase in adult perception of the LEGO build experience as a creative tool, not just a child's toy. The LEGO Group reported a 30% uptick in adult-targeted product sales in the UK within six months following the campaign, clearly showing that Fervor sells.

**How to Build Fervor**

So, how do brands ignite this kind of Fervor? How do they not only enter but also steer the cultural conversation? It's about more than just being seen; it's about being spoken of, becoming a topic at dinner tables, a reference in tweets, a hashtag in the ever-swirling maelstrom of social media discourse. It's about finding a resonant chord and strumming it with just the right rhythm - here's how you do it.

*Step 1: Be Worth Talking About*

First, if you want people to talk about your brand, give them something to talk about. This isn't about gimmicks or cheap tricks. This is about finding the soul of your brand and letting it scream. It could be a revolutionary product, a groundbreaking service, or a campaign that touches nerves or tickles ribs. Make sure whatever you do, it's not lukewarm—nobody talks about lukewarm. And remember, Fervor is nothing without emotion. Whether it's joy, surprise, or even outrage, tap into these primal forces. Emotional content is shared content. It's the laugh, the tear, the jaw drop that gets passed along from user to user, across platforms, transcending the digital realm into coffee shop conversations.

*Step 2: Tell the Right Story*

People don't just share products; they share stories. Find the narrative thread that ties your brand to something bigger. Is it a story of rebellion, of overcoming odds, of innovation, or of simple pleasures? Craft this story well, embed it in every message, every campaign, every piece of marketing collateral. Make it simple, make it resonate, and make it so damn compelling that they can't help but repeat it. And be authentic. Nothing kills fervor like a brand that tries too hard to be what it is not. If you're a gritty, rough-around-the-edges kind of brand, own it. People respect authenticity and can smell a fake from a mile away. Authenticity fosters trust, and trust breeds fervor.

*Step 3: Use the Megaphones*

In today's digital bazaar, virality is partly science, partly art, and a whole lot of luck. Tap into the megaphones—social media influencers, brand advocates, and die-hard fans. Equip them with the story and let them amplify it. Choose those who resonate with your brand's values and have the audience's ear. When they talk, people listen. When they listen, get them involved. Whether it's through user-generated content, challenges that spread like wildfire, or simply asking for opinions, make interacting with your brand as fun as throwing darts in a dive bar. Reward participation, spotlight the best contributions, and keep the energy high.

*Step 4: Keep the Home Fires Burning*

Consistency is key in keeping the conversation alive. You can't just spark fervor and walk away. Keep feeding the fire with fresh content, ongoing engagements, and continual innovation. This isn't about bombarding them; it's about keeping them eagerly waiting for what's next. Always leave them wanting more. Whether it's a cliffhanger at the end of a campaign, a teaser of what's next, or an unfinished challenge that beckons the brave, never let the story end too neatly. Keep them on their toes, guessing and wanting more.

*Step 5: Celebrate the Cult*

Once you have a following, nurture it. Celebrate it. Build exclusive groups, offer insider access, make members feel like part of the brand family. They're not just followers; they're evangelists, they're part of the gang. Give them the badges, the secret handshakes, and the first dibs on new offerings.

Building brand fervor isn't for the faint of heart. It's for the bold, the brave, and the slightly mad. It's for those who believe that their brand can be a living, breathing part of culture—a topic of dinner conversations, the muse of memes, and the heart of hashtags. So, roll up your sleeves, and start making noise. The kind of noise that can't be ignored.

As we wrap up our exploration of the F-Factors of Fame, we've journeyed through Familiarity, Favorability, Feeling, and now Fervor. Each factor builds upon the last, creating a comprehensive framework for understanding how brands capture hearts and minds. But remember, while Fame sets the stage, it's Flow that completes the dance.

## *Findability: Navigating the Digital & Physical Realms*

Let's dive into the trenches of Flow, starting with its first cornerstone: Findability. This isn't just about being seen; it's about being found precisely when and where it matters most. In the fragmented universe of consumer choices, physical and digital availability isn't just a convenience—it's a strategic imperative.

Findability transcends the simple notion of visibility. It intertwines with both physical presence and digital prowess, becoming a dual force that places products within arm's reach of desire, both virtually and tangibly. Amazon reengineered this concept, turning shopping from a passive activity into a proactive discovery, making it almost an ambient presence around us. This giant doesn't just sell products; it redefines and dominates the pathways to purchase by embedding itself into our daily digital interactions.

During the COVID-19 pandemic, Aperol recognized a seismic shift in consumer behavior—a spike in at-home drinking. Traditional routes to the consumer through bars and physical retailers were choked by lockdowns, thrusting the brand into a direct-to-consumer (DTC) play. This wasn't a mere shift but a radical transformation in distribution strategy. Aperol retooled its approach to Findability by diving deep into SEO, not just to appear but to dominate search terms linked to at-home drinking solutions, capturing new territories in organic search rankings with a staggering 94% increase.

Working hand-in-glove with SEO experts, Aperol's journey exemplifies the evolution of Findability from a passive condition to an active strategy. Brands are compelled to navigate the digital topography, not as bystanders but as shapers of the consumer pathway. They sculpt their presence with the precision of seasoned artisans, ensuring they appear not only at the right place but precisely when their audience is poised to buy.

Tubi's stunt during the 2023 Super Bowl is another masterclass in modern Findability. In a move that blurred the lines between reality and advertisement, they 'hacked' the UX of viewers' smart TVs. The seemingly accidental switch to Tubi's app was a deliberate ploy, cleverly engineered to boost app visibility and intrigue. This gimmick didn't just increase app opens—it catapulted Tubi into the spotlight, achieving the highest search rate in its history and demonstrating the power of creative disruption in a crowded media space.

But Findability isn't confined to grand gestures or large platforms. It manifests in every nuanced interaction that guides a customer to a product. It's the breadcrumbs on the digital path leading Hansel and Gretel not to a witch's lair, but to premium shelf space and top search results. It's about understanding the algorithmic undercurrents that sway product rankings and the strategic placements that intercept consumer journeys.

From the physical shelves in stores where packaging design fights for consumer attention, to the digital battlegrounds of e-commerce where algorithms determine product fate, Findability is the art of ensuring your product is both seen and chosen. It demands an astute understanding of consumer habits and marketplace dynamics, leveraging every tool from SEO to sophisticated market analytics to ensure that when a consumer looks for a product, yours appears as if it was always meant to be found.

## Initiative Case Study in Findability:
*Ring's Memorial Day Moment of Truth*

For a long time, Ring stood as the reigning champion of home security. But the world is a rough place, filled with contenders hungry to take down the king. A findability analysis laid it bare: 34% of Ring's paid search was gasping for air, underperforming, a number that jabbed at the gut because when you're the leader, everyone's trying to knock you off your perch.

Ring had to perfect the search strategy by Memorial Day, ahead of their 'Super Bowl of Sales'... Prime Day. Their objective was to push efficiency and effectiveness to new levels during their May Memorial Day sales campaign to ensure Ring had the right strategy ready in time for Amazon Prime Day in July.

Could Generative AI, that mysterious beast lurking in the shadows of the marketing world, be the strategic ally Ring desperately needed? While the ivory tower types were still debating AI's potential impact, Ring was already putting it to the test. They weren't just going to use AI; they were going to make it bleed gold.

By the time AI became the talk of the town in March 2023, Ring had already been in the trenches with it. ChatGPT had undergone a rigorous "training camp," and was now ready to be thrust into the starting lineup of Ring's search strategy. It wasn't just about using AI—it was about forging a new weapon.

They flipped the script on AI prompts. Instead of just pushing deals and discounts, they dug into the bedrock of human motivation. The AI was prompted to weave cultural and categorical truths into the copy, betting on depth over discounts. It wasn't just fed data; it was schooled in the art of war. Tailored for Responsive Search Ad (RSA) formats, the AI had to understand the strict parameters and search best practices that had been hard-won over years of digital battles.

The stage was set. Memorial Day was not just another sales day; it was Ring's proving ground. The campaign, fueled by AI-crafted copy, was a departure from the norm. It was faster, sharper, and more efficient. The AI slashed the time spent on crafting ad copy by 40%. What used to be hours of human deliberation was now done in minutes, freeing up precious resources for strategic maneuvers. The click-through rates soared by 172%. It was the digital equivalent of a moonshot, proving that when you speak to the heart, the clicks will follow. The cost-per-click plummeted by 73%. Each dollar was now working not just harder, but smarter. Direct-to-Consumer unit sales shot up by 32% year-over-year. The numbers were singing, and they were singing Ring's tune.

The AI-driven strategy wasn't just a temporary patch; it was a revolution. The majority of Ring's search copy was now chiseled by AI, paving the way for plans to integrate AI into social media strategies through dynamic creative optimization.

### How to Build Findability

In a world cluttered with information and as many brands as there are stars in the sky, making your brand stand out becomes a question of survival. How do you make sure your brand pops up like a beacon, whether someone's scrolling through their phone or walking down the street? Here's the raw, straight shot on making your brand findable.

### Step 1: Understand the Terrain

Before you can dominate the landscape, you need to understand it. That means mapping both the physical and digital realms where your brand needs to shine. Physically, where do your customers hang out? Digitally, what are they searching for? This is about knowing your audience inside out—what they eat for breakfast and what keeps them up at night.

### Step 2: Master the Art of SEO

SEO isn't just a marketing buzzword; it's the path you lay down to lead customers to your door. Start with keyword research. Find out what your audience is typing into that all-knowing search bar when they're looking for services or products like yours. Tools like Google Keyword Planner or Ahrefs can give you insights into search volumes and keyword difficulties. Your job? Integrate these keywords seamlessly into your website's content, from blog posts to the product descriptions, making sure it's as natural as breathing. Content is king in SEO. Your content should serve by answering questions, providing solutions, or just making life a little easier. Start a blog, create videos, or start a podcast—whatever fits your brand persona and appeals to your audience. Make your content helpful, interesting, and shareable. This builds organic traffic and establishes your brand as an authority in your field.

### Step 3: Become a Wizard of SEM

While SEO is your long game, SEM (Search Engine Marketing) is your quick draw—the ads you pay for to jump to the front of the line in search results. Google Ads can be your best friend here if you handle it right. The key is crafting ads that speak directly to the pain points and desires of your audience while also leveraging the keywords you uncovered in Step 2. Be precise, be clear, and most importantly, be compelling.

## Step 4: Optimize Your Website for Humans and Bots

Your website is your digital storefront, and just like a physical store, accessibility matters. Ensure that your website is a place where both search engine bots and human beings love to visit. This means having a clean, navigable design, fast load times, and content that answers questions instead of just shoving sales pitches down visitors' throats. Mobile optimization isn't optional anymore, considering most searches happen on those little screens we carry everywhere. Backlinks—other websites linking to yours—are like votes of confidence in the eyes of search engines. But not all votes are equal. Focus on building relationships with reputable partners whose content can naturally link back to yours. Guest post on reputable sites, be active and helpful in online communities related to your industry, and always provide value before asking for anything in return.

## Step 5: Get Local, Get Physical

Findability in the physical world means making your presence known locally. If you have a physical location, tools like Google My Business are invaluable. Keep your listings up to date with addresses, phone numbers, and operating hours. Encourage satisfied customers to drop a review. Sponsor local events or host workshops. Make your brand a visible and active member of your community.

Building your brand's findability is about being as visible as possible, but it's also about being genuine in how you present yourself. Make sure that when they find you, they remember you.

## *Facilitation: Smoothing the Path to Purchase*

Facilitation—the art of smoothing the passage through the consumer lifecycle—isn't just about paving the road; it's about removing the roadblocks, smoothing out the bumps, and sometimes, when the path is too tangled, laying down a whole new road.

Take the mundane but essential task of improving site navigation or simplifying sign-up processes. It sounds technical, like the kind of problem that needs a squad of developers to decode. Yet, sometimes, the most effective solutions are stark in their simplicity.

Consider McDonald's, a behemoth in the fast-food industry, known for its keen sense of what drives consumer action. When McDonald's aimed to boost their app downloads, they didn't just request it—they made it irresistible. The promise was straightforward: download the app and enjoy free fries every Friday for the rest of the year. It's a simple, clear incentive that aligns perfectly with their customer base's desires. Who wouldn't tap download for a free serving of fries?

This example underscores a vital element of Facilitation: incentives matter. It's not always about overhauling systems or investing in high-tech solutions. Sometimes, it's about providing a clear, tangible reason for customers to overcome the inertia of inconvenience.

However, addressing Facilitation requires a granular understanding of the customer experience. Every touchpoint, from the moment they land on your website to the instant they decide to make a purchase, must be scrutinized for potential improvements. This involves mapping out the customer journey in its entirety and identifying every possible friction point that could deter a customer.

One friction point often overlooked is research overload—paralysis by analysis. Customers today are bombarded with information, options, reviews, and comparisons. Making a decision in such a saturated space can be overwhelming. Brands that manage to simplify this decision-making process gain a significant competitive edge. A streamlined, curated experience that guides the customer gently but firmly towards a decision can dramatically enhance the effectiveness of your marketing funnel.

Customer service, too, plays a crucial role in Facilitation. It's the safety net that catches customers before they fall through the cracks of dissatisfaction. It's about ensuring that when things go wrong, resolution is quick, painless, and, ideally, exceeds expectations. In the age of social media, a customer's frustration can quickly escalate into a public relations crisis, while a well-handled complaint can transform a disgruntled buyer into a brand advocate.

The importance of price as a barrier cannot be understated. Pricing strategies must be transparent and perceived as fair. Hidden charges, complex discount schemes, or just plain high prices are all hurdles that can deter a purchase. Here, the key is clarity—help your customers understand what they're paying for and why it's worth it.

In essence, Facilitation is about removing obstacles, making it as easy as possible for the customer to say yes. It's about enhancing every aspect of the customer journey to make it more efficient, more enjoyable, and ultimately, more effective at driving sales.

**The Ultimate Facilitation Story**

In the labyrinth of life's tedious tasks, few endeavors elicit as much dread as tax season. The mere mention of tax preparation sends shivers down the spines of many, conjuring images of endless forms, confusing jargon, and the looming specter of potential errors. However, amidst this bleak landscape of financial responsibility, there exists a beacon of hope – TurboTax.

TurboTax, the unsung hero of tax season, transforms the arduous task of tax preparation into a surprisingly delightful experience. It's not just about the end result; it's about the journey – a journey that TurboTax masterfully guides users through with its intuitive and rewarding user experience.

From the moment you embark on your tax-filing odyssey, TurboTax greets you with open arms, beckoning you into its digital realm with a user interface so inviting, even the most tax-averse souls find themselves drawn in. With its seamless navigation and user-friendly design, TurboTax ensures that even the most complex tax forms feel as manageable as a stroll through the park.

But TurboTax doesn't stop at merely holding your hand through the process. Oh no, it goes above and beyond to make you feel like a tax-filing champion at every turn. With each deduction you uncover and credit you claim, TurboTax showers you with praise, celebrating your financial acumen like a proud mentor applauding a student's success.

Yet, TurboTax's genius lies not only in its ability to reward users for their progress but also in its knack for turning mundane tasks into moments of triumph. As you input your financial information, TurboTax diligently calculates your potential refund or tax liability, transforming the abstract concept of numbers on a screen into tangible rewards or warnings. It's like watching your own personal financial narrative unfold before your eyes, complete with twists, turns, and hopefully, a happy ending.

But what truly sets TurboTax apart is its expert use of cutting-edge UX technologies to elevate the tax-filing experience to new heights. Through seamless integration of AI-driven assistance, personalized recommendations, and real-time feedback, TurboTax anticipates your needs, guides you through the process, and empowers you to take control of your financial destiny like never before.

As you traverse the tax-filing journey with TurboTax as your trusty guide, you can't help but feel a sense of accomplishment with each step forward. It's as if TurboTax is whispering in your ear, encouraging you to keep going, assuring you that the end is near, and the reward is well worth the effort.

In the end, TurboTax is more than just a tax-filing software; it's a testament to the transformative power of exceptional user experience. Through its seamless interface, constant encouragement, and expert use of technology, TurboTax has succeeded where many have failed – making the most boring job in the world not only bearable but downright enjoyable. TurboTax has made Facilitation a foundational principle for their entire product offering. But Facilitation can also be a very powerful marketing tool, especially in eCommerce where new digital platforms can transform the way people buy.

## Initiative Case Study in Facilitating Crime Fighting:

*Dutch Police S.I.M*

In 2023, nearly 20% of Dutch citizens claimed to be victims of crime—a 3% jump in just one year. The police, drowning in cases, couldn't keep up. Their numbers were among the lowest per capita in Europe, and they were buried in unsolved files. Traditional methods—like knocking on doors—were outdated and ineffective. They needed tips from witnesses, but reaching the right people in time was a nightmare. Eyewitnesses can crack a case wide open, but they had to act fast. The smallest detail, shared promptly, could mean the difference between catching a crook and letting the trail go cold. The problem was, many witnesses didn't even realize they'd seen something important.

That's when the Dutch Police turned to performance marketing. The same tools that facilitate the consumer's path to purchase a brand's products were now repurposed to facilitate the path to solving crimes. It was a radical shift: using marketing channels not to sell, but to protect and serve. We built a system that could turn media algorithms into a crime-fighting powerhouse. Enter Special Investigative Media (S.I.M.).

When a crime happened, the police logged it into their system. Within minutes, hundreds of digital assets targeted the local population—right down to the zip code. Calls to action urged potential witnesses to share their tips on the police's website. The AI-powered system analyzed the crime data—location, time, severity, images, surveillance footage—everything. It then created customized ads for each case. Depending on what was available, these ads could include maps, CCTV images, witness videos, or just text.

Using hyperlocal targeting, the system deployed assets across platforms like Google, Microsoft, Facebook, Instagram, and Snapchat. The police force's messages hit the screens of the right people, exactly when needed, pushing them to report what they may have seen. If a case dragged on, the assets updated with new details from the police or fresh tips from the public. Once solved, the campaign stopped. Case closed, thanks to media.

Special Investigative Media created a more efficient police force with a deeper connection to the public and activated the most powerful public safety network ever assembled, with over 450,000 citizens clicking on the assets and 500 cases solved and counting. The Dutch Police increased their investment by 25% and even created a new role: Special Investigative Marketer. We didn't just harness the power of media to keep citizens safe. We rewrote the playbook on crime-solving, one digital ad at a time.

**How to Build Facilitation**

Facilitation is like lubricating a rusty door hinge. It's about making sure once your customer grabs the handle, the door swings open effortlessly, without a squeak. It's about making the buying process not just easy, but downright enjoyable. Here's how to grease those skids so well that your customers slide right from "just looking" to "just bought."

*Step 1: Know Your Customer's Journey Like Your Own Backyard*

First things first, map out the customer journey. You need to understand every twist and turn from discovery to purchase. This is about knowing where your customers come from (search engines, social media, direct visits) and where they hit potholes. Use tools like Google Analytics or customer feedback to trace this path. Never stop looking for feedback. Listen to what your customers are telling you. Not just in the reviews they leave, but in the data—where do they drop off during the buying process? What are they complaining about? Use this feedback to make immediate improvements. This continuous loop of feedback and enhancement can turn a good buying experience into a great one.

*Step 2: Cut the Crap*

Every extra step in your checkout process is a hurdle. Every unnecessary form field is a pitfall. Simplify it. If you're asking for their second cousin's middle name, you're doing it wrong. Streamline your forms to ask only what's necessary. This might mean name, contact info, payment details, and that's it. The faster you let them get from "I want this" to "I bought this," the better.

*Step 3: Make Your Website a Smooth Operator*

If your website is slow, you've got a problem. Speed it up. Optimize images, leverage browser caching, and reduce server response time. Your website should load faster than it takes for their second thoughts to kick in. Make navigation intuitive. No one should need a map to find your products or the checkout button.

*Step 4: Opt for Omnipresence*

Be where your customers are. If they hang out on Instagram, have a shop set up there. If they use Facebook, make sure your store is integrated. Utilize platforms like Shopify or WooCommerce to synchronize your inventory across all these channels. This omnipresence makes it easier for them to buy no matter where they are.

*Step 5: Communicate Like a Human, Not a Robot*

Your customers are people. Talk to them like it. This means customer service that's as real and raw as it gets. No scripted responses or cold corporate lingo. Use live chat tools, manned by real people, or at least well-trained AI that doesn't sound like it's stuck in the '80s. Be available. Be helpful. Be human. And anticipate what they want. If you know that customers often buy a certain type of battery with a certain type of gadget, suggest it at checkout. Anticipating their needs can make the buying process feel personal and thoughtful, and saves them the hassle of a return visit or a second order.

## *Fascination: The Art of Capturing Hearts & Minds*

Fascination is where engagement meets magic. It's not just about getting your message in front of people; it's about creating content that captivates, that pulls people in and keeps them coming back for more. This is about delivering the right message, through the right channel, at precisely the right moment.

Consider the innovative approach taken by Skinny in New Zealand—a telecom brand that turned a lack of advertising funds into a community-driven campaign phenomenon. Facing the challenge of budget constraints, Skinny did something most brands wouldn't dare: they invited their customers to create the content. By asking their audience to call in and record parts of their radio ads, they engaged their base in an unprecedented way. With 2,500 of their 250,000 customers participating, they achieved a remarkable level of engagement. The recordings weren't just for radio either; they were printed on coffee cups, plastered across newspapers, and featured in out-of-home advertisements. This wasn't just a campaign; it was a mass mobilization of consumer creativity, turning traditional advertising on its head and fostering a deep, community-driven connection to the brand.

Such campaigns show the power of media and creative synergy. It's essential to consider how these elements can work together to maximize the relevance and impact of your communications. At the core of this synergy is the strategic placement of ads—understanding where and when they can generate the most attention and ensuring they resonate deeply with the intended audience.

The focus on attention has become more pronounced, with many brands hotly pursuing new ways to measure how captivated their audience truly is. We're probing the depths of attention metrics, exploring how they can inform our media strategies and enhance ad receptivity. The idea is to align our content not just with the eyes of any viewer but with those who are most likely to engage deeply with the brand.

This brings us to a critical junction in the conversation about Fascination: the challenge of fleeting exposures. In an era where digital distractions are a dime a dozen, the reality is that attention spans are short and getting shorter. The goal, then, isn't to hijack attention unethically but to earn it respectfully and effectively. This perspective shifts the strategy from capturing attention briefly to building memorable, engaging experiences that leave a lasting impression.

✦ ◆ ✦ ◆ ✦ ◆ ✦ ◆

### Initiative Case Study:
*Fascination Echoes in the Deep South for Gilead*

The Pharma space is arguably the toughest category for creating fascination – as compelling, lean-in content about public health, diseases and prescription drugs is hard to digest. Gilead Sciences, a leader in the battle against HIV, faced a formidable challenge. In the American Deep South, a region shadowed by longstanding cultural norms and deep-seated stigma, conversations about HIV are nearly nonexistent. Public health messages are often ignored or outright rejected, buried under layers of fear and misinformation. The need was clear: to bring these critical discussions into the open, making them as much a part of the Southern dialogue as church on Sunday mornings.

Understanding the unique cultural landscape of the South—where stigma around sexuality and healthcare runs deep—Gilead aimed to dismantle these barriers. Their goal was not just to inform but to transform the conversation about HIV into one of hope and collective resilience. But achieving this meant engaging with the community in a manner that felt safe, familiar, and respectful of their deeply rooted values.

Enter "In the Deep," a custom podcast designed to penetrate these barriers using the intimate and accessible format of audio storytelling. Hosted by Zach Stafford, a native of the region with a personal connection to the cause, the podcast planned to weave the real-life experiences of individuals directly affected by HIV into a narrative that spoke to and from the heart of the Southern states. The journey of "In the Deep" was more than just a podcast; it was a cornerstone of a larger, strategic campaign designed to shift the cultural conversation about HIV in the South. This ambitious project hinged on personal stories that resonated deeply within the community, employing a medium that was both discreet and direct.

Recognizing the importance of privacy in these discussions, Gilead Sciences chose audio as the primary medium. This choice was based on compelling data indicating that 60% of Black and Latinx men in the South, who were significantly affected by HIV, already engaged with podcasts and other audio formats for information. In the past three years alone, the number of Black consumers using podcasts had increased by 70%. Audio allowed listeners to explore sensitive topics in the privacy of their own space, creating a safe environment for engagement and reflection.

The podcast featured a series of in-depth discussions with guests ranging from people living with HIV to activists and social justice advocates. Each episode was crafted to explore themes such as trauma, identity, forgiveness, self-love, and community solidarity—themes that resonated on a personal level with the listeners.

Each episode was a slice of life, delivered through the gravelly voices of locals who had lived through it all and come out the other side. These weren't polished tales; they were the kind with rough edges and raw, exposed nerves. Gilead and Zach Stafford rolled out episodes that weren't just facts and figures but real, gritty stories—people talking about lives torn and stitched back together, about love found in the cracks of brokenness, about finding forgiveness in places they were taught to hate.

To amplify the reach and impact of the podcast, Gilead Sciences implemented a comprehensive media strategy that included both terrestrial and digital streaming audio across a vast radio network. Trusted voices from local communities were enlisted to deliver host reads, enhancing the authenticity and relatability of the messages. Custom email newsletters, tailored social media posts, and digital amplification strategies were deployed to ensure that the message of "In the Deep" permeated through the targeted regions. This personalized approach helped to build a community around the podcast, encouraging ongoing dialogue and engagement on a level that traditional public health campaigns could not.

The real measure of success wasn't just in the metrics—though the millions of impressions and hundreds of thousands of downloads told a story of their own—but in the quiet victories: a young man walking into a clinic, a mother hugging her son a little tighter after listening to an episode, a preacher mentioning the podcast from the pulpit in a tentative bridge between faith and health.

"In the Deep" became more than just a campaign. It was a testament to the power of storytelling, a proof that even in places heavy with old ghosts and older habits, a good story could still turn heads and maybe, just maybe, hearts too.

As the campaign unfolded, the engagement metrics began to reveal the depth of its impact. The podcast garnered nearly 100 million impressions and hundreds of thousands of downloads, but more importantly, it motivated nearly 50,000 individuals in the targeted communities to seek HIV testing and sexual health services. This marked a significant achievement in a region where health disparities had long been the norm.

"In the Deep" proved to be more than just a campaign; it was a movement. By leveraging the power of storytelling and the intimacy of audio, Gilead started a conversation that many thought impossible in the conservative strongholds of the American Deep South. Through each episode, each story, they chipped away at the stigma surrounding HIV, encouraging individuals to step forward, get tested, and engage in open conversations about their health. The narrative around HIV in these communities was changing, paving the way for a future where public health and personal dignity walked hand in hand.

### How to Build Fascination

So how do we build Fascination, the siren call that draws the customer deeper into the brand's narrative, binding them with stories told well and told memorably?

### Step 1: Know the Room

What does your audience want? A break from the mundane? A shot of wisdom? Understanding their content needs is crucial. Dig into their behaviors, likes, dislikes, and pains. Use surveys, social listening tools, or dive into data analytics. Know them better than they know themselves.

### Step 2: Map the Content Journey

You've mapped your customer's journey. Your content needs to light the path at every stage. Tailor your content to answer their questions before they ask them, solve problems they didn't know they had, and tickle their curiosity at just the right moment. Mapping your content journey lets you place the right signposts along the way.

### Step 3: Serve the Good Stuff

Quality beats quantity. Every piece of content should add value. Think utility, entertainment, or enlightenment. It's not just about what you want to say, but what they need to hear. Make your content the answer to their Google searches, the comfort in their chaos, the laugh during their lunch break.

### Step 4: Get Personal

If content is king, personalization is the crown jewel. Segment your audience and tailor your messages. Use data to personalize at scale—think dynamically customized emails, content recommendations, or personalized landing pages. Make them feel like you're the bartender who remembers their usual.

*Step 5: Engage, Don't Preach*

Interaction deepens engagement. Involve your audience with polls, quizzes, or UGC (user-generated content) challenges. Turn passive readers into active participants. When they engage, they invest emotionally, and when they invest emotionally, they're hooked.

Creating content that fascinates isn't just about filling up your website or spamming feeds. It's about crafting experiences, stirring emotions, and making your brand unforgettable. Like the best nights out, the ones that resonate are the ones that feel personal, are full of good stories, and maybe, just maybe, teach you something new in the process.

### *Following: Building Bonds That Last*

We've reached the final turn in our exploration of the Fame & Flow model, staring down the often overlooked yet crucial concept of Following. This isn't just about accumulating numbers; it's about cultivating real, lasting relationships with your customers, owning those connections without the middleman of third-party platforms.

Following is fundamentally about building bonds—both functional and emotional—with those who buy into your brand. Functional ties might involve exemplary customer service, innovative loyalty programs, or a customer experience that consistently exceeds expectations. Emotional bonds, however, delve deeper, tapping into the psyche and resonances of your consumer base.

Consider Nike, which has mastered the art of exclusivity with its limited-edition sneaker drops. This strategy doesn't just sell shoes; it cultivates a dedicated community of sneaker enthusiasts, individuals who feel a profound connection to the brand through shared passion and exclusivity.

Delta Air Lines presents another facet of following, evolving from near bankruptcy to a titan of the skies, largely through its SkyMiles program. Delta cultivated such a robust following that it recently found itself recalibrating the very loyalty program that propelled its resurgence, striving to maintain the quality of service that its frequent flyers expect.

Then there's Peloton, which transcended its identity as a fitness equipment manufacturer to become a central hub of community and cult-like zeal. Peloton's rise was fueled by its interactive classes, charismatic instructors, and a fiercely loyal online community that transformed workouts into social, shareable events.

When dissecting campaigns that effectively build following, the utilization of data to foster community engagement stands out. Spotify's Wrapped campaign is a textbook example, transforming user listening habits into a celebration of personal taste and shared experiences. Each year, Wrapped not only recapitulates users' musical journeys but also integrates opportunities for deeper interaction, such as direct links to purchase artist merchandise. This approach not only enhances user engagement but also promotes social sharing and brand advocacy, turning personal milestones into public celebrations.

However, cultivating following isn't merely about leveraging data or creating exclusivity. It's about recognizing and nurturing the human element of business. It's about understanding that behind every transaction, there's a person seeking to connect, to be seen, and to belong.

✦ ◆ ✦ ◆ ✦ ◆ ✦ ◆

**Initiative Case Study:**
*How the Canadian Down Syndrome Society bridged the employment gap by building a new following*

In 2023, there was a troubling paradox at the heart of North America's labor market. They were faced with a historic job shortage of nine million unfilled positions and employers in desperate need of hard-working and reliable employees. At the same time, more than half of Canadians with Down syndrome, eager and ready to work, were sidelined and struggling to find meaningful paid employment.

For many people with Down syndrome, employment is a critical step towards building independence. Despite a long-standing history of being valuable contributors in a variety of industries, the Down syndrome community still suffered from outdated stereotypes and misconceptions about their capabilities and were being ignored by potential employers.

The Canadian Down Syndrome Society (CDSS) exists to bridge the gaps in support and resources that make life unnecessarily tough for people with Down syndrome. Their work with employers identified that even those willing to hire are often clueless about where to start or how to connect with jobseekers with Down syndrome.

Enter Inployable, a groundbreaking initiative born from a partnership between CDSS and LinkedIn. This first-of-its-kind employment network for people with Down Syndrome was designed to help prospective employers connect with potential employees and access resources like training processes and inclusive hiring practices.

Creating Inployable wasn't straightforward. LinkedIn's platform doesn't allow for aggregating job seekers from specific communities. So, hyper-targeted social posts were used to invite members of the Down syndrome community to join Inployable via a simple form – and they were effectively employed by Inployable, which was set up as a company page on LinkedIn. This strategy not only gave these individuals an optimized LinkedIn account but also boosted their visibility in job searches.

The campaign launched with a powerful video during Canadian Down Syndrome Week, featuring individuals with Down syndrome advocating for their right to work. This call to action drove both employers and job seekers to the hub, building connections that would otherwise be missed.

To enhance the discoverability of these candidates, over 30 new skills were added to the platform to more accurately reflect the strengths of the community. For those needing extra help, live one-on-one sessions with a LinkedIn Coach were provided.

Next, LinkedIn data was used to identify major corporations across Canada with relevant job openings, and in partnership with the Captivate elevator network, CDSS served ads in those office buildings, calling out companies by name and introducing them to Inployable candidates.

Despite limited resources, Inployable has thrived. The campaign has amassed over 149 million impressions, shattering stereotypes and raising awareness about the invaluable contributions of people with Down syndrome. In just two months, the platform has built a rich following of over 700 people across 164 industries, with 91% of those followers working directly in HR. LinkedIn has lauded Inployable as one of the fastest-growing company pages on the platform. Most importantly, Inployable has been helping candidates secure employment, and making a meaningful difference in the lives of those with Down syndrome.

**How to Build Following**

There are brands—and then there are *legends*. You want to be the latter, trust us. A brand with a loyal following isn't just selling a product or a service; it's selling a piece of immortality. How do you transform your brand from just another name to a sacred mantra on the lips of your consumers? Here's a how-to guide, cut straight to the bone.

*Step 1: Know your Die-Hards*

First, you've got to know your die-hard fans. Who are these people? What cracks them up, what ticks them off, and what gets them out of bed in the morning? This isn't about demographics and data points; it's about understanding them like you understand your own flawed self. Get under their skin, feel their pulse. This is the cornerstone of everything that follows. Make sure you get their details. You're going to want to spend a lot of time with them. Your audience will also evolve, and so should you. Stay curious about them, about the world they live in, about the waves that rock their boats. The more you understand them, the better you can serve them. This isn't just about market research; it's about caring, about maintaining a relationship that's alive and kicking.

*Step 2: Create Exclusivity*

Not the snobbish kind, but the kind that makes people feel like they are part of something special, something unique. Limited edition products, members-only content, insider perks. Give your followers the VIP treatment and make them feel like insiders in a world full of outsiders. This isn't just about making them feel special—it's about making them feel chosen.

*Step 3: Engage, Don't Broadcast*

Throw out the megaphone and get a seat at the table. Engagement is the secret sauce of building a following. Respond to comments, start conversations, ask questions, stir up a debate. Get involved. Social media isn't a billboard; it's a cocktail party. Be the guest everyone wants to talk to, not the one shouting over everyone else.

*Step 4: Reward Loyalty Like Your Life Depends on It*

Because, in a way, it does. Your lifeblood as a brand is the people who come back time and again, who defend and advocate for you. Find ways to reward them, whether through loyalty programs, shoutouts, or simply by letting them know they are seen and appreciated. Make loyalty the best business decision they ever made.

*Step 5: Face Your Screw-Ups Like a Champ*

You're going to screw up; it's inevitable. When you do, face it head-on. Apologize, make it right, and move on. How you handle mistakes can cement a follower's loyalty more firmly than a hundred successes. This isn't just damage control—it's an honesty that's rare and refreshing in a world that's too full of fine print.

As we reflect on the power of Following, the question becomes: How can you activate your own fan base to amplify your brand? It's not just about creating fans; it's about empowering them, giving them the tools and the reasons to champion your brand to others. Whether it's through exclusive offers, insider information, or simply making them feel like part of the family, when you activate your followers effectively, they become more than customers—they become your most effective marketers.

As we close this chapter on Following, remember that each of the F-Factors of Flow—Findability, Facilitation, Fascination, and Following—interconnects to create a comprehensive strategy for growth. Together, they form a framework that not only attracts but also retains, not just catches the eye but captivates the heart.

## *Fame x Flow: The Twin Engines of Growth*

Fame and Flow are not just complementary; they are interdependent. Like the flame and air of a hot-air balloon, one lifts the brand up while the other keeps it soaring. Together, they drive brand growth not only in the immediacy of today but also sustain it over the long haul, supporting not just direct sales but also enhancing pricing power, distribution, and market penetration.

The concept of Fame has been bandied about in marketing corridors for decades, swinging wildly from being an elusive target measured by vague metrics to being a concrete goal driven by digital clicks. But as we've evolved, so too has our understanding of Fame. It's not just about awareness; it's about achieving a status where a brand becomes a staple of conversation, both online and offline. It is the art of becoming not just recognized, but revered.

Fame acts as the great amplifier. It increases the demand ceiling, allowing brands to not just enter markets but expand them. It creates a reservoir of goodwill that brands can draw on in times of crisis or competition. Fame is not just about being known; it's about being known for something worthwhile.

If Fame is the flame, Flow is the air that keeps the balloon aloft. It is everything that happens after the flame catches—how a brand guides potential customers towards making a purchase, how it exceeds their expectations, how it fits seamlessly into their lives, and how it turns them into advocates. Flow is about creating a friction-free experience that aligns with the consumer's needs, desires, and expectations.

In today's digital age, Flow extends beyond traditional sales and marketing channels to encompass a broader spectrum including retail media, owned properties, and more. It is about making every touchpoint along the customer journey an opportunity to enhance the consumer's experience and relationship with the brand.

Imagine Fame and Flow as a dance, a complex ballet where each supports and enhances the other. Fame draws them in, Flow keeps them moving smoothly. Without Flow, Fame is just a hollow echo, a brand everyone knows but no one buys. Without Fame, Flow struggles to engage, like a well-oiled machine operating in a vacuum.

For CEOs and marketers, understanding and harnessing the interplay between Fame and Flow is crucial. It allows them to direct marketing budgets with precision, ensuring that each dollar spent is not just an expense but an investment in building a brand that not only exists in the market but dominates it.

**Testing the Fame x Flow Model**

We started with the hypothesis that Fame and Flow, these twin sirens, sing in harmony to seduce growth out of the market's chaos. But we need proof, raw data that could either crown or crucify our beliefs. So we researched, putting numbers to a theory, bringing quantitative clarity to a qualitative world.

To give legs to our theory, we dipped into comprehensive data lakes: YouGov BrandIndex for consumer sentiment and brand perception, and Ahrefs for digital visibility and engagement metrics. Together, these platforms offered a wide lens on brand performance across various dimensions. The Fame x Flow model uses these datasets to create a composite view of brand health and growth potential.

You can find the details of the analysis in the Appendix. The crux of it began with assigning measurable indices to the conceptual components of Fame (Familiarity, Favorability, Feeling, and Fervor) and Flow (Findability, Facilitation, Fascination, and Following). Each factor was linked to specific data points that could reflect real-world behaviors and outcomes. For instance, Fame's familiarity was closely tied to unaided brand recall, while Flow's facilitation connected with customer reviews citing ease of purchase.

Our data spanned several continents and industries—from automotive giants in Germany to quick-service restaurants in Australia—ensuring that our findings had both depth and breadth. Each category brought its own set of challenges and insights, making our analysis robust and nuanced.

*Here are the key findings.*

*1. Independent and Interdependent Forces of Growth*
Both Fame and Flow independently correlate with growth (GKPI). Brands with high Fame scores showed significantly more growth than less famous counterparts. Conversely, high Flow scores also propelled growth independently.

*2. Amplifiers of Each Other*
We split brands into terciles based on their Fame and Flow scores, then watched how changes in one affected the effectiveness of the other. Brands swimming in the high-Fame pool saw Flow's impact on growth nearly

double compared to those paddling in the shallows of low Fame. It turns out, being well-known isn't just about getting nods in the street; it makes every dollar spent on smoothing the customer journey work harder. We also saw that high Flow increases the effectiveness of Fame by 60%. So they amplify each other. Brands that enjoy high levels of Fame benefit even more from improvements in Flow, and vice versa. It's a dance of mutual benefit, a give-and-take that spins the wheels of growth faster.

*3. Consistency Across Borders and Industries*

The Fame x Flow effect held true across different markets and categories, validating the model's universal applicability. However, nuances did exist—some categories like leisure and retail showed more elasticity in Fame's impact on Flow, suggesting that the consumer's buying cycle and the nature of the product influence the interaction between Fame and Flow.

*4. The Bigger Brand Advantage*

Larger, more established brands leveraged Fame to a greater extent than smaller brands. This finding was pivotal for strategic planning, indicating that while emerging brands should focus on building Flow to enhance customer experience, they must not neglect the gradual construction of Fame to maximize long-term growth.

The implications of our findings are profound. Brands must think of Fame and Flow not as isolated silos but as intertwined elements of a single strategy. A dual investment strategy ensures that brand efforts are not just creating buzz but also paving the way for real, measurable growth.

So far we've talked about Fame and Flow—a system designed not just to attract glances but to forge and nurture connections. We've dissected its components, the F-factors, and laid out the map through which brands can navigate their growth. We have also shown that while Fame and Flow are your lead dancers, how well they perform together dictates the success of the show and the legacy it leaves. We quantified the success and uncovered the 4 laws of Fame and Flow. Now, it's time to roll up our sleeves and dive into crafting your own Fame and Flow blueprint, the master plan to elevate your brand from the crowd, to make it something people not only notice but follow devoutly.

## CHAPTER 4

# BUILDING FAME & FLOW

## *Crafting Your Fame & Flow Blueprint*

It's not enough to just recognize the dual engines of Fame & Flow; brands must actively engage in designing a strategic blueprint that leverages these concepts for tangible growth. This chapter peels back the layers of the Fame & Flow Blueprint, a tactical guide that brands can use to assess, enhance, and capitalize on their market positioning.

The Fame & Flow Blueprint isn't just a strategic tool; it's a diagnostic framework that evaluates a brand's current performance against a set of established benchmarks—the F-factors of Fame and Flow. It scrutinizes how a brand stacks up against its competitors in these critical areas, identifying both strengths to be leveraged and weaknesses to be addressed.

The goal? To outline a clear and actionable path that aligns marketing efforts with the most effective growth levers, ensuring that every marketing dollar spent is an investment towards measurable growth.

### 1. Diagnose: The Quantitative Assessment

The first phase of the blueprint involves a comprehensive diagnostic assessment, where brands are quantitatively scored across each of the eight F-factors. This phase employs a mix of consumer surveys, digital analytics, market data, and competitive analysis to paint a detailed picture of where a brand stands. Imagine, for instance, a brand in the athletic apparel sector. The diagnostic might reveal high scores in Familiarity and Favorability but lower ratings in Flow aspects like Facilitation and Following. This indicates a strong brand presence that isn't fully capitalizing on customer journey optimization or post-purchase engagement.

## 2. Audit: The Deep Dive

Following the diagnosis, the blueprint moves into the audit stage. This is where data turns into narrative. The audit involves a deep-dive analysis, looking at the historical context, the current market dynamics, and the competitive landscape. It's about understanding why certain F-factors are underperforming and how they're interrelated. For our athletic apparel brand, the audit might uncover that while the brand is popular, its online shopping platform is not as user-friendly as its competitors', leading to lost sales. The audit provides a narrative that explains not just what is happening, but why it's happening, laying the groundwork for targeted interventions.

## 3. Prioritize: The Strategic Focus

The final phase is prioritization. Here, the learnings from the diagnosis and audit are synthesized into a clear set of priorities. This is where the structural equation modeling comes in, identifying which F-Factors have the most substantial impact on growth within the specific context of the brand's market and competitive environment. For our example, if the data shows that improving Facilitation and Following could lead to significant growth, those factors become the priority. The prioritization phase culminates in a strategic roadmap that outlines specific, actionable steps for enhancing these key areas, complete with KPIs and timelines for execution.

Implementing the Fame & Flow Blueprint means transitioning from theory to practice. It involves setting up cross-functional teams to tackle the prioritized F-factors, aligning budget allocations to support these initiatives, and continuously monitoring progress against the strategic goals. In essence, the blueprint transforms the abstract concepts of Fame and Flow into a concrete, operational strategy that brands can execute.

## *Diagnosing Fame & Flow: The First Critical Step*

Diving deep into the Fame & Flow model begins with a rigorous diagnostic phase. This initial step is critical as it quantifies the present state of a brand across the spectrum of Fame and Flow, employing the eight F-Factors as a framework. Our approach to diagnosis is twofold, involving both bespoke and standardized methods. Here, we primarily explore the standardized route, using public data sources to benchmark a brand against its competitors and across industries. We favor a combination of both approaches in practice to capture a nuanced, accurate representation of brand performance.

The standardized method hinges on leveraging data from established, accessible sources. YouGov BrandIndex emerges as a primary tool due to its comprehensive global reach and the depth of its data across diverse market segments. YouGov's metrics provide a solid foundation for measuring each of the F-Factors systematically. This approach allows not only for an evaluation of a brand's standing but also enables robust competitor and industry benchmarking.

With these metrics defined and data gathered, the next step involves detailed analysis to understand not just where the brand stands, but also its trajectory over time and its position relative to competitors. This analysis helps identify strengths to build upon and weaknesses that need strategic attention.

This standardized diagnostic approach, while offering a broad comparative perspective, is complemented by bespoke metrics tailored to the unique aspects of a brand's operations and market dynamics. Together, these methodologies furnish a robust, dynamic view of a brand's performance, guiding strategic decisions in the subsequent stages of the Fame & Flow Blueprint.

To show how telling our Fame & Flow Diagnostic can be, let's examine one brand that's seen its fair share of ups and downs in recent years: Tesla, and compare it to two stable, long-standing titans: BMW and Mercedes-Benz. We'll start by traveling back in time to 2020, looking specifically at United States General Population.

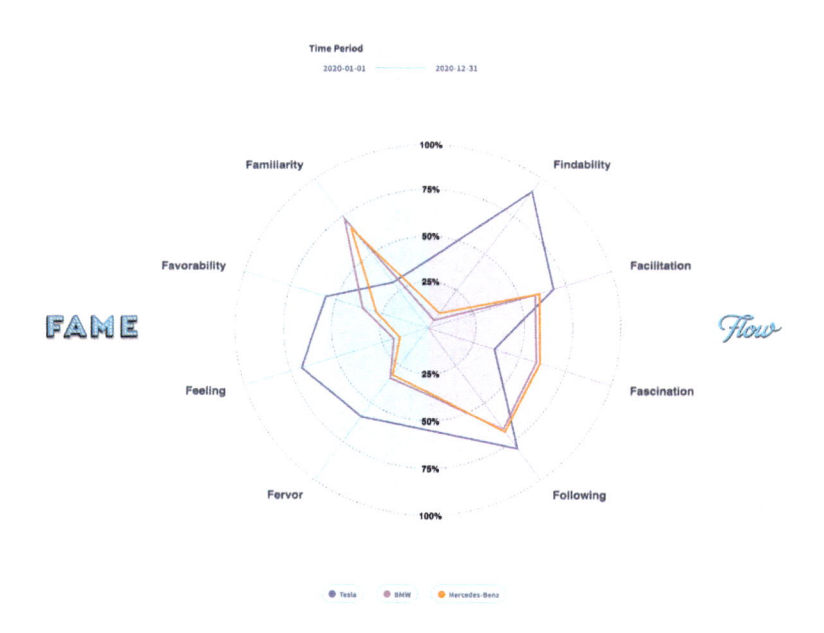

From here, we can make some fast, off-the cuff observations. First, Mercedes-Benz and BMW are competing neck and neck in all F-Factors, while Tesla shines as a true outlier. How come?

Tesla's 2020 was marked by exceptional business performance: a soaring stock price and substantial profits reinforced its leadership in both the electric vehicle and luxury space. Not surprisingly, Tesla excelled in most of the 8 F-Factors, but notably in these four:

- **Favorability:** At this time, Tesla is known not only as one of the most advanced electric vehicles on the market, but as a status symbol more generally, driving brand preference and product consideration.

- **Feeling:** Tesla's dominance in the electric vehicle space, as well as its prominence in the news, culture, and entertainment, helped keep the brand top of mind, owning mental availability.

- **Fervor:** Media coverage largely celebrated Tesla's resilience and innovation. There were rumblings about Elon Musk's controversial Tweets, but that negative Fervor was still in the early stages, and as this radar suggests, had yet to impact brand perceptions.

- **Findability:** Tesla's bet on its direct-to-customer sales model was a risky one, as the brand could not rely on a vast dealership network to drive physical and digital availability. But this risky move paid off and proved critical during the early pandemic, as they were able to continue to sell while brick-and-mortar dealerships shuttered their doors around them. Their bold expansion of production in Shanghai, Berlin, and Texas in the months prior significantly boosted Tesla's product availability during the year 2020. Meanwhile, its competitors Mercedes-Benz and BMW (among others) fell victim to vast supply chains slowdowns.

Tesla's weakest F-Factors were Familiarity, given its newness to the market compared to its long-standing competitors, and Fascination, linked to ad engagement—unsurprising with zero spend on paid media.

Now, let's fast forward four years to the first quarter of 2024. Elon has since bought Twitter amid massive controversy, his public persona becoming more exaggerated, bizarre, and unfiltered. The company's reputation for constant innovation has wavered with little product newness in the market with one exception: the very delayed Cybertruck (which launched to mixed reviews). Further, a slew of critics has started to call out the brand for poor build quality and rushed testing. How did this impact Tesla across its Fame & Flow Score?

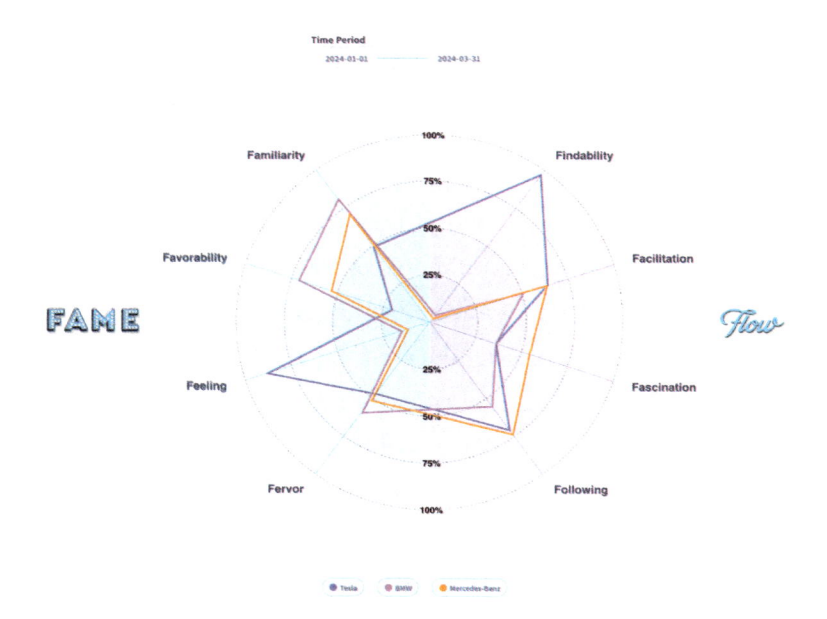

Primarily in - you guessed it - Favorability. Tesla saw a 62% drop in Favorability in four years. The once EV darling is now stained, no longer the desirable, premium savior of the auto industry.

Surprisingly, we see a dip in Fervor too. Elon, not Tesla, is what is on the tip of everyone's tongue. He sucked up not all, but a significant amount of the brand's oxygen.

And, if one wasn't yet convinced that Fame & Flow is intrinsically tied to growth, perhaps this Fortune headline from April '24 might do the trick: *"Tesla will try to stem the bleeding on its earnings call after its worst sales quarter in four years, a round of price cuts, and a sinking share price."*

The Diagnose step, thorough and rigorous, is more than an exercise in measurement—it's the foundation upon which strategic action is built. It informs every subsequent decision in the Fame and Flow blueprint, guiding brands on where to focus their energy to maximize growth and impact.

### The Fame & Flow Audit: Unveiling the Story Behind the Scores

Having navigated the initial diagnostics of the Fame & Flow model, the next critical phase is the Audit. This stage is where raw data and quantitative metrics begin to tell the deeper stories of a brand's engagement and effectiveness in the marketplace. The Audit isn't just about crunching numbers; it's a discerning examination of the narrative behind the digits. It's about peeling back the layers of surface data to unveil the qualitative nuances that influence brand performance.

The Audit phase is designed to offer a comprehensive review of a brand's current standing across all eight F-Factors, as established in the diagnostic phase. It delves into the strengths and weaknesses of the brand, provides insights into competitive positioning, and identifies strategic opportunities for growth. The goal is to translate quantitative findings into actionable insights that inform strategic marketing decisions.

*Questions to Unearth the Narrative*

#### FAME FACTORS

- **Familiarity:** How does your brand's Familiarity stack up against competitors? Are there demographic variations? Perhaps a new product or a sub-brand is lagging in recognition. Here, tools like YouGov provide a snapshot, but diving into client-supplied data or brand trackers can offer deeper nuances.

- **Favorability:** What drives your brand's Favorability? Are there shifts in consumer sentiment? Leveraging YouGov alongside social listening tools can reveal the dynamic interplay of brand values and consumer perceptions, tracking how these evolve under competitive pressures.

- **Feeling:** What immediate associations do consumers have with your brand? Are your marketing efforts creating the desired mental availability? This exploration can benefit from AI tools that analyze general perceptions, providing a proxy for the widespread emotional engagement with your brand.

- **Fervor:** How is your brand's Fervor manifesting in social conversations? Are you a part of the trending dialogues within your industry? Measuring word-of-mouth and social engagement through competitive lenses helps identify both the momentum and the potential gaps in your social strategy.

## FLOW FACTORS

- **Findability:** Where does your brand appear in organic searches? Who dominates the digital shelf? Understanding the visibility in both digital and physical realms, through tools like search rankings, can highlight opportunities to enhance your presence where it matters most.

- **Facilitation:** What are the common barriers that hinder customer progression through the buying cycle? Analyzing customer journey maps and identifying friction points relative to your competitors can spotlight areas needing strategic intervention.

- **Fascination:** Are your marketing efforts translating into traffic and engagement? This factor requires evaluating the effectiveness of your ads and content through metrics like ad awareness and brand interaction, possibly utilizing marketing mix modeling or attention metrics to fine-tune your approach.

- **Following:** Does your brand enjoy a robust community of advocates? Understanding aspects like Net Promoter Score (NPS) and customer loyalty, alongside the general sentiment in social discussions, can provide insights into the strength and health of your brand's community.

Each element of the audit phase is aimed not just at understanding where a brand stands but also at shaping the strategic direction it should take. By merging quantitative data with qualitative insights, we create a rich, multi-dimensional portrait of the brand's current market position and its potential trajectories. This holistic approach ensures that every strategic recommendation is grounded in a deep understanding of both market dynamics and consumer behavior.

## *Prioritization: The Art of Selective Focus in Fame & Flow*

After gathering rich data and diving into the audit, the journey through the Fame & Flow blueprint reaches a crucial stage: Prioritization. This isn't merely about understanding what each F-Factor signifies; it's about discerning which of these F-Factors are pivotal to boosting your brand's market trajectory.

Prioritization is the analytical core of the Fame & Flow blueprint, determining which F-Factors are not just underperforming but crucial for driving significant business outcomes. It's about aligning strategic focus with empirical evidence to ensure that marketing investments are not just well-intended but surgically effective.

To sift through the complex interplay of F-Factors and business outcomes, we employ structural equation modeling (SEM). SEM allows us to see beyond simple correlations; it helps us understand how multiple aspects of Fame and Flow interact in a dynamic system, influencing each other and ultimately business performance.

Think of SEM as the analytical lens that brings the hidden relationships into focus. It quantifies the strength and direction of relationships between variables, offering a clearer picture of where investments could yield the most significant returns. Imagine you're analyzing a tech company struggling to improve its market position. Our SEM might reveal that while Familiarity and Favorability are important, Fervor (the degree of passionate advocacy or buzz around the brand) has the most substantial direct effect on increasing customer acquisition rates.

## STRUCTURAL EQUATION MODEL SHOWCASES
## THE POWER OF EACH FACTOR BEHIND FAME & FLOW

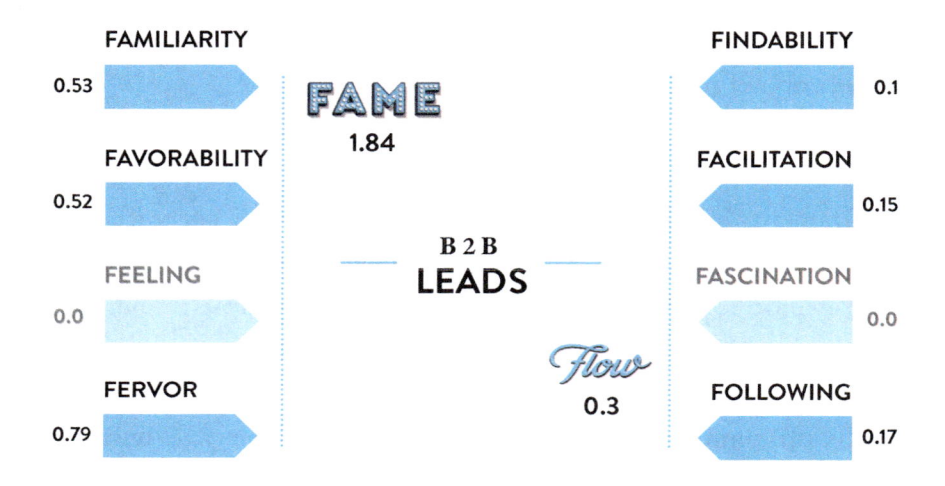

| | | | |
|---|---|---|---|
| FAMILIARITY | | FINDABILITY | |
| 0.53 | **FAME** | | 0.1 |
| FAVORABILITY | **1.84** | FACILITATION | |
| 0.52 | | | 0.15 |
| FEELING | **B2B** | FASCINATION | |
| 0.0 | **LEADS** | | 0.0 |
| FERVOR | *Flow* | FOLLOWING | |
| 0.79 | 0.3 | | 0.17 |

Prioritization through SEM isn't just a statistical exercise; it's a strategic imperative. It allows marketers to craft interventions that are not just precise but also aligned with the overarching goals of sustained business growth. In this complex interplay of F-Factors, SEM acts as the compass that guides marketers through the murky waters of strategic decisions, ensuring that every dollar spent is an investment toward measurable and meaningful growth.

## CHAPTER 5

# FAME & FLOW AS A CHANGE AGENT

## *Breathing New Life into an Old Concept: Integration*

Fame and Flow, this new model we're proposing, is not just about driving growth; it's about driving change. As we peel back the layers of what we've discovered, we find that its implications stretch far beyond mere metrics and models; they herald an entirely new way in how we approach everything in our industry—from crafting brand strategies to media investment, from the mobilization of our talent to the very structure of our operations.

Let's break it down into three distinct areas where Fame & Flow will not just influence but will actively reshape our approaches: Integration, Simplification, and Experimentation.

In today's marketing landscape, a crucial, though often overlooked, ailment has persisted: disintegration. This isn't just about departments working in silos or the left hand not knowing what the right is doing; it's deeper. It's about a fragmented approach to delivering marketing services, each fragment operating with its own agenda, language, metrics, and even, fundamentally, its own conception of what marketing is supposed to achieve. This age-old disintegration has been the quiet saboteur of potential synergies that could propel brands to new heights.

It is here that the Fame x Flow model presents an opportunity, a lifeline to pull marketing out of this fragmented morass by advocating for a new level of integration. This is not merely about streamlining operations—it's a radical rethinking of how every facet of marketing can be interwoven to enhance the overall impact of each marketing dollar spent.

The call for integration is clear: to maximize the utility of our marketing investments, we must bridge the gaps between disparate marketing functions. This goes beyond the simple coexistence of creative and media, extending to an orchestrated synergy between all elements that contribute to a brand's Fame and its Flow. It means aligning market research, digital strategies, customer service, content creation, media buying, and analytics under a unified strategy that leverages insights from each to optimize the others.

Consider this: a brand invests heavily in media to boost brand awareness but neglects customer service, leading to poor customer experiences that undermine potential gains in brand reputation and customer loyalty. Here, the disconnect between media spend and customer experience creates a leak in the marketing bucket, where the efforts to fill it (Fame) are undermined by holes (poor Flow) that drain it.

Achieving integration requires a comprehensive redesign of operational approaches. It demands that marketing leaders view the orchestra of paid, owned, and earned media not as separate tools but as interconnected instruments that play together to produce a harmonious symphony of brand growth. This involves integrating customer experience directly into the marketing fold, considering it not as an afterthought but as a central component of the marketing strategy.

The trend toward in-housing media operations is a testament to brands' growing recognition of the need for greater control over and integration of their marketing efforts. However, true integration goes beyond the mere location of operations and into the essence of how these operations are conceived and executed. Whether operations are in-house or outsourced, the key is to ensure that they are not isolated but are part of a strategic whole.

This requires a level of partnership between agencies and clients that is deeply strategic. Agencies must not only deliver on specified services but must understand and integrate into the broader business objectives of their clients. They must evolve from service providers to strategic partners, offering insights that span across traditional service boundaries.

Integration's success hinges on the ability to measure and understand its impact. This involves developing metrics that can capture the cross-functional impacts of marketing activities. How does an improvement in customer service metrics influence brand perception? How does increased brand awareness impact customer acquisition costs or customer lifetime value?

By developing and tracking these integrative metrics, organizations can begin to see not just the direct outcomes of specific initiatives but the interplay between different areas of marketing and business operations. This approach not only provides a more comprehensive view of marketing's effectiveness but also highlights areas where further integration could yield significant returns.

As we move forward, the call for integration is not just a suggestion—it is an imperative. The future of marketing lies in our ability to break down the old barriers and build new bridges. In this future, marketing is not a department but a central, integrative force driving business growth through strategic, coordinated action across all fronts. This is the path to not just surviving but thriving in the competitive landscape of tomorrow, where integration is not just an advantage but a necessity.

## *Simplify, Simplify, Simplify*

Complexity has become a beast of burden for our industry. The landscape is littered with disparate metrics and overwrought dashboards, with the effectiveness of marketing efforts often obscured by the very tools meant to illuminate them. The issue is not just about measurement but interpretation and communication—translating marketing efforts into language that resonates beyond the marketing department and into the boardroom.

The Digital Marketing Association (DMA) threw a stark light on this issue with a report that dissected the metrics used across 1,000 marketing campaigns submitted for their awards since 2017. The findings were an avalanche of data points—170 distinct metrics, with a shocking 41% labeled as "vanity metrics," those alluring numbers that, despite their glitter, tell us little about business impact. Only a slender 6% could be considered "business metrics," those that connect directly with the core objectives of a company.

This gap between what is measured and what matters is not just a marketing dilemma; it's a business challenge. The investment community has started to tune into the rhythm of branding as a driver of business growth. A revealing survey by the IPA highlighted the evolving perspective of both sell-side and buy-side analysts. Here are the harmonics of this new tune:

- A robust 75% view marketing as an investment, not a mere cost.

- A commanding 89% believe marketing expenditures should be capitalized, at least partially.

- Brand strength and marketing prowess topped the chart of factors analysts consider when evaluating publicly listed companies, surpassing even leadership quality and reported profit.

- Marketing's importance was underscored by 79% of analysts, ranking it above sustainability and ESG concerns.

These perspectives herald a significant shift in how marketing is perceived in the high-stakes world of finance. Yet, this is not merely about recognition—it's about reclassification. The idea that marketing should be treated as an intangible capital expenditure rather than a simple operating expense speaks to a fundamental shift in understanding its role in generating long-term value.

The challenge for marketers is dual: first, to internalize and then to articulate the direct link between marketing initiatives and business performance. This is not just about ensuring that marketing metrics are aligned with business KPIs but also about educating those within and outside the organization about the strategic value of marketing.

Marketing must therefore transcend its traditional boundaries and become a central part of the business conversation. This involves a deep understanding of how the business generates revenue and profits and how marketing contributes to these processes. Questions like the cost-effectiveness of selling a product through various channels, the contribution margin by channel and SKU, and the overall efficiency of marketing tactics must be answered not just within marketing teams but across the enterprise.

For CMOs, the imperative is clear: they must not only champion the complexity of marketing's contribution to growth but also simplify how this is communicated to ensure clarity and impact. The C-suite must be fluent in the language of marketing, appreciating not just the tactical but the strategic value that marketing brings.

The Fame x Flow model emerges as a beacon in this cluttered landscape, offering a framework that balances simplicity and depth. It provides a narrative that is both comprehensive and comprehensible, linking everyday marketing activities to strategic business outcomes. By focusing on measurable impacts—those that can be articulated in the boardroom and defended in the market—this model does not just aim to convince but to convert understanding into action.

The journey from complexity to simplicity is not about stripping away the nuances of marketing but about enhancing its clarity and impact. As marketers, the task ahead is to mold our strategies and metrics not just to reflect the changing landscape but to lead it. In this way, marketing does not just respond to business needs but reshapes them, offering a clearer, more compelling narrative of growth that resonates from the boardroom to the marketplace.

## Never-ending Experimentation: Constantly x Consistently

Why do giants of the digital era like Netflix, Amazon, and Booking.com launch thousands of experiments each year, fine-tuning everything from webpage layouts to service offerings? This isn't indulgence; it's necessity. In a world where consumers demand uniquely tailored experiences, and economic pressures squeeze budgets, these companies use experimentation not as a luxury, but as a survival tool.

Today's landscape is a minefield of vanity metrics that dazzle but rarely deliver, masking the essential figures that could genuinely steer a company toward prosperity. Despite the data deluge, most big brands engage in experimentation with a timidity that borders on the ceremonial, rarely achieving the scale or depth needed to draw meaningful business conclusions. They peck at the surface, confined by brand silos and geographical constraints, often failing to measure the ripple effects throughout the marketing funnel.

Enter the strategic experimenters—those rare breeds who've cut through the fluff to anchor their tests to solid business objectives. They aren't just running tests; they're seeking to elevate their marketing effectiveness by substantial margins or to fuel double-digit growth. This isn't about confirming preconceived notions but about challenging every assumption with rigor, supported by a comprehensive approach that scrutinizes everything from click-through rates to actual sales.

Coca-Cola gets it. It slices its budget pie like this: 70% goes to the no-sweat, surefire stuff—the daily grind; 20% gets a kick of old magic dusted off for another round; and the wild 10%? That's thrown at the new, the untried, the 'what the hell' ideas. They mix the safe bets with the gambles, crafting a strategy that keeps them steady on their feet while they stretch their arms out for the next big catch. That's how Coke plays it—smart money with just enough crazy to keep things interesting.

Or take Allianz. Stuck with a blurry view of their marketing's effectiveness, they set up a lab of sorts, crafting an AI-enhanced model to test how their ad dollars translated into policies on the ground. In one bold move, they cranked up social media spending in select regions and watched how it played out across the marketing funnel. The result? A 25% boost in effectiveness, proving that when you align your experiments with real business outcomes, the returns can be intoxicating.

As digital cookies crumble under the weight of privacy laws and consumer skepticism, marketers are forced to get creative with how they track and measure conversions. It's no longer sufficient to rely on the old methods; it's time for experimental design, market mix models, econometrics, and controlled tests. Adjusting budgets and mixes, probing different media channels, and dissecting every piece of data—this is the alchemy of experimentation in modern marketing.

Experimentation isn't just a solo act; it requires a band. Successful companies know this, orchestrating across global stages, harmonizing efforts from local dives to international arenas. They empower their local squads with the tools to set up, run, and learn from experiments in real time, feeding insights into a global database that tunes the whole company's strategy.

Many brands are terrified of this kind of experimentation. It's risky, it's messy, and it often doesn't pan out. But those who do embrace this chaos find gems hidden in the rubble. They discover tactics and strategies that not only work but catapult their brand into the stratosphere of market relevance. Failure is a gift here, because, in this game, the sting of a flop is a lesson bought in blood and dollars. Each failed experiment, each misguided campaign, isn't just a blot on a marketer's record—it's a notch on the belt, a scar to show and tell. From these failures, we learn, refine, and dare again. The true value of the Fame x Flow model lies not only in its successes but in its splendid failures.

# CLOSING TIME

We wrote this book because we saw the crisis, felt the quake of an industry shuddering under the weight of its own illusions. Marketers everywhere are starting to feel it. A slow, simmering realization that something's profoundly off. We've been diagnosing the wrong symptoms with the wrong tools, believing we've got it all figured out just because everything's measurable now. This digital age handed us a ruler, a stopwatch, and a calculator, and told us, "Go ahead, measure everything." And like good little marketers we did, because who doesn't like things that are neat and quantifiable?

But just because it's measurable doesn't mean it's meaningful. We fell for it, hook, line, and sinker. We adopted outdated mental models like the marketing funnel and brand versus performance, thinking we were cutting-edge. Digital platforms nudged us gently, sometimes not so gently, down this path because, let's face it, when we spend more on short-term performance marketing, their pockets get deeper. It's a slick game where everyone on the outside wins—CEOs and corporate boards love it because the numbers look clean and logical, and CMOs get to keep their jobs because they're seen as driving "results."

But this isn't just a game. This is a crisis. While we've been busy measuring, we've missed the essence of how marketing really works. We never stopped to ask the critical questions. We took the models handed to us and ran with them without wondering if they were the right ones or if they even made sense anymore.

In this book we set out to answer that gnawing question: How does marketing really work? We introduced a new mental model—Fame & Flow—not just as a concept, but as a robust, resilient framework that aligns with the latest thinking in psychology and marketing academia. But this model isn't just academic; it's practical, designed to be understood and used across your organization to explain what marketing really does.

We tore down Fame into its core components: Familiarity, Favorability, Feeling, and Fervor. Each element critical, interconnected, feeding into the notion that brand awareness isn't just about being seen—it's about being remembered, loved, felt, and fervently talked about.

Then, we dove into Flow with Findability, Facilitation, Fascination, and Following, showing how these elements ensure that once your brand is loved, it's also easy to find, engage with, and buy.

Our proprietary research proved that Fame and Flow don't just drive business results on their own; they amplify each other, echoing across markets and geographies, resonating in a symphony of sustained success.

We walked you through how to build your own Fame & Flow blueprint, starting with a diagnosis to understand where you stand, moving through an audit to dive deeper into your brand's narrative, and ending with a prioritization mechanism that doesn't just scatter your efforts but sharpens them, focusing intensely on what really moves the needle.

And we covered the big changes this model will usher in. The Fame & Flow framework demands a new level of integration within your marketing teams. It calls for a simplification of the complex metrics we've been tangled up in, cutting through the clutter to reveal what's truly important. And it champions a relentless commitment to experimentation—because what's marketing if not a grand experiment in human psychology and behavior?

As you close this book and look towards your own marketing horizons, remember that applying the Fame & Flow model isn't just about following steps; it's about embracing a philosophy. A philosophy that respects the complexity of human desires and the simplicity of clear communication.

The Fame & Flow model isn't a map but a compass; it won't show you every turn, but it will ensure you're headed in the right direction. So take this model, shake up the system, stir the pot, and make some noise. You'll need to be nimble, brave, and a little reckless - the good kind of reckless that questions every 'truth' and tests every boundary.

Let Fame & Flow be your guide. May your brand's voice echo across the digital expanse, not as a whisper but as a roar. May your strategies not just meet targets but move hearts. And may your journey through the chaotic world of marketing lead to a place where your brand isn't just seen or heard, but followed and favored.

Here's to your success, to your courage, and to your unyielding spirit. May Fame & Flow light your path. Cheers, to a future redefined.

# APPENDIX

# DETAILED RESEARCH FINDINGS

**Testing the Fame x Flow Model**

For our research, we first needed to populate the Fame x Flow model with data. We used two main sources: YouGov BrandIndex and Ahrefs. To test the validity of the Fame x Flow model we correlated the data with a proxy KPI for customer growth (GKPI) – for this we used YouGov Current Customer. This is the percentage share of the survey's sample that owned or purchased the brand.

YouGov and Ahrefs data were chosen for a variety of practical reasons, but importantly because they are normalized databases of consumer research that cover many regions and categories, afford us huge numbers of data points, and allow for a consistent time series analysis.

The constituent parts of Fame x Flow were assigned proxy measures primarily from the YouGov database. Fame was mainly sourced from YouGov while Flow was a mixture of data from YouGov and Ahrefs. We ran myriad analyses to test the Fame x Flow model. We wanted to know how well it would stand up to scrutiny and/or would need to be modified as we learned more about how Fame, Flow, and their constituent parts behaved in real-world situations.

To that end, we analyzed data from the US, Germany, Australia, and from across several categories: Automotive (non-luxury cars), CPG (carbonated beverages), Durables (consumer electronics), Leisure (QSR restaurants) and Retail (athletic apparel).

In the Appendix we have placed a detailed description of the statistical analysis that we performed, including confidence limits.

## The Findings: How Fame x Flow Drive Growth

We present here the findings of the statistical analysis we performed on measures of Fame, Flow and their eight constituent parts (the eight Fs).

Our main finding is that the Fame x Flow model and its link to growth is proven by the numerous sets of analysis that the team performed across thousands of calculations involving millions of data points. To put our conclusion simply:

To maximize growth, a brand needs both Fame & Flow. Fame & Flow are clearly linked and must be considered as a pair of variables that interact and influence each other. Brands with equivalent Fame grow faster if they have higher Flow and brands with equivalent Flow grow faster if they have higher Fame. The model holds true across countries and categories.

These conclusions are supported by the following four central findings:

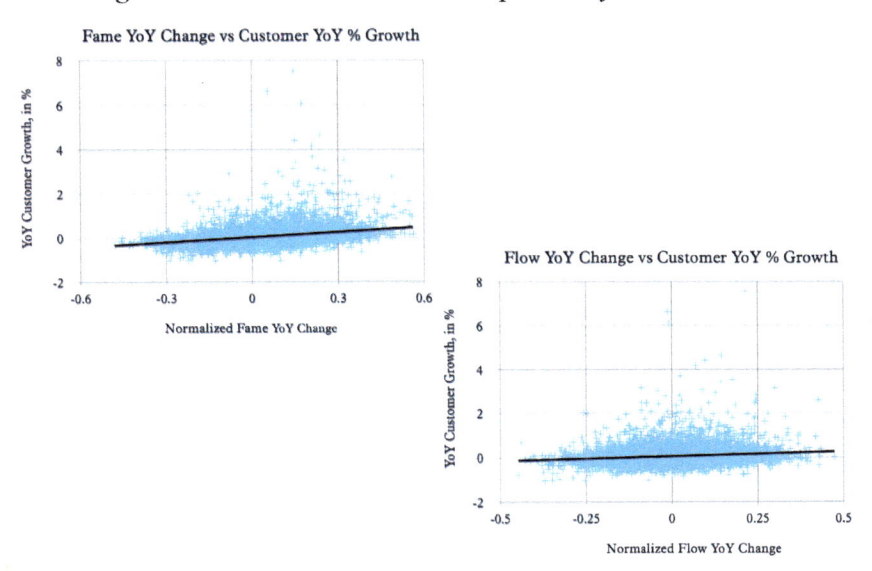

*Fig.1 Both Fame and Flow Act Independently to Drive Growth*

### 1. Fame & Flow Can Each Act Independently to Drive Growth

While Fame & Flow are not the only contributors to a brand's growth, both Fame (+0.37) and Flow (+0.17) are statistically important and correlated to growth. From the graph, it is also evident that changes in Fame have more impact on growth than changes in Flow.

As a brand gets incrementally more famous, it tends to grow more than when compared with the same incremental improvements in, say, the customer journey. Scale confers its own advantage. We went further and examined the data to see how a 1 percentage point change in Fame or Flow would affect the GKPI. The table below expresses the graphs in a simpler format.

| CHANGE IN FAME OR FLOW (%) | GROWTH IN GKPI (%) | GROWTH IN GKPI (%) AT 90% CONFIDENCE LIMITS |
|---|---|---|
| 1% INCREASE IN FAME | 1.32% | 1.325% +/- 0.015% |
| 1% INCREASE IN FLOW | .32% | 0.36% +/- 0.015% |

*Fig 2. As Fame increases, the strength of Flow's connection to growth improves*

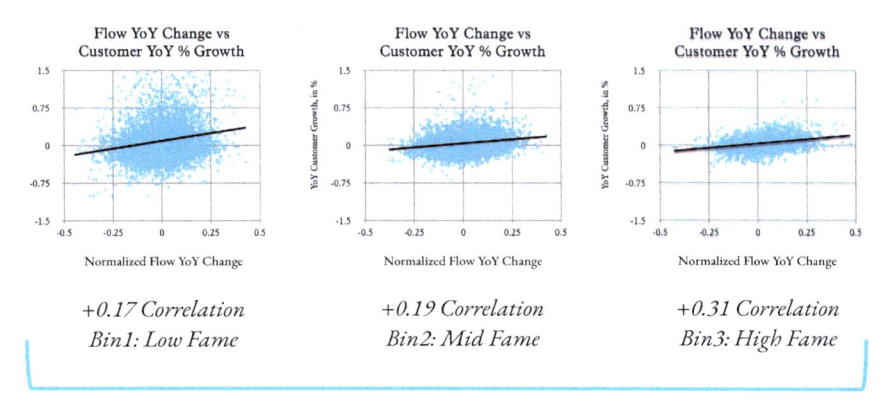

+0.17 Correlation
Bin1: Low Fame

+0.19 Correlation
Bin2: Mid Fame

+0.31 Correlation
Bin3: High Fame

## AS FAME INCREASES, THE STRENGTH OF FLOW'S CONNECTION

*Fig. 3 As Flow increases, the strength of Fame's connection to growth improves*

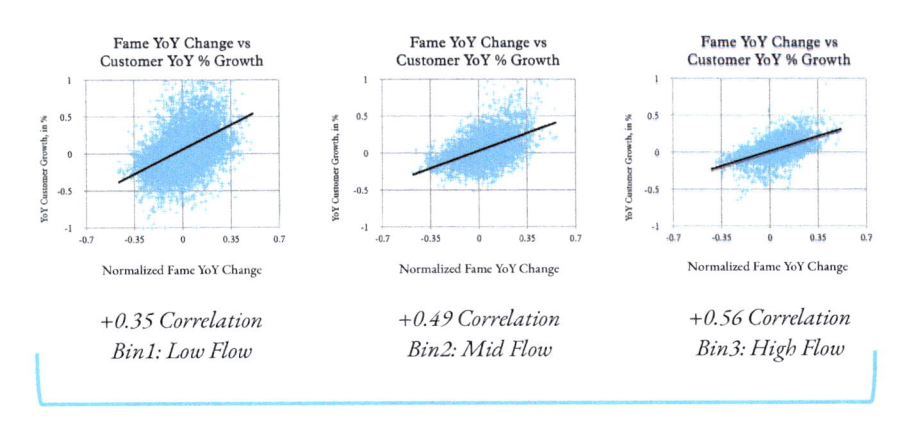

+0.35 Correlation
Bin1: Low Flow

+0.49 Correlation
Bin2: Mid Flow

+0.56 Correlation
Bin3: High Flow

## AS FLOW INCREASES, THE STRENGTH OF FAME'S CONNECTION TO GROWTH IMPROVES

## 2. Fame & Flow Act as Accelerators of Each Other and Drive Brand Growth

We sorted brands according to their absolute Fame values - within a specific country and category, brands were grouped into one of three further categories, by tercile: low, mid, or high Fame. The correlation within each group was then calculated between Fame & Flow growth versus the percentage growth of the GKPI.

We found that Flow is correlated to the GKPI, but the effect is more pronounced for brands with more elevated levels of Fame. As Fame increases there is a catalyzing effect on how improvements in Flow connect to brand growth. The strength of Flow's connection to customer growth nearly doubled (0.17 vs 0.31) for brands in the high Fame bin relative to those in the low Fame group. This means that the impact of Flow (optimizing the customer experience and journey) is even stronger when brands are already well-known and mentally available in the category.

Brands were then grouped differently —this time according to their absolute Flow values, by tercile. Within a specific country and category, brands were grouped for either having low, mid, or high Flow. As before, Flow has a catalyzing effect on Fame's connection to growth. The strength of Fame's connection to growth increases, with higher Flow, as indicated by the higher correlation values. Fame's correlation to customer growth improved by approximately 60% (.35 vs .56) for brands in the high Flow group vs those in the low Flow group. This means that the impact of Fame (brand-strengthening efforts) is even higher when more optimal customer journeys are in place.

*Fig.4 The correlation between normalized Fame and Flow YoY growth vs. Current Customer YoY growth for each bin level and by market*

**Australia**

Flow YoY Change vs Customer Growth: 0.18, 0.19, 0.30

Fame YoY Change vs Customer Growth: 0.39, 0.50, 0.53

**Germany**

Flow YoY Change vs Customer Growth: 0.17, 0.20, 0.42

Fame YoY Change vs Customer Growth: 0.30, 0.49, 0.62

**US**

Flow YoY Change vs Customer Growth: 0.19, 0.20, 0.25

Fame YoY Change vs Customer Growth: 0.37, 0.52, 0.53

Bin1 ■ Bin2 ■ Bin3

**CORRELATION BETWEEN NORMALIZED FAME X FLOW YOY GROWTH VERSUS CURRENT CUSTOMER YOY GROWTH IN % FOR EACH BIN LEVEL, BY MARKET**

*Fig.5 The correlation between normalized Fame and Flow YoY growth vs. Current Customer YoY growth for each bin level and by category*

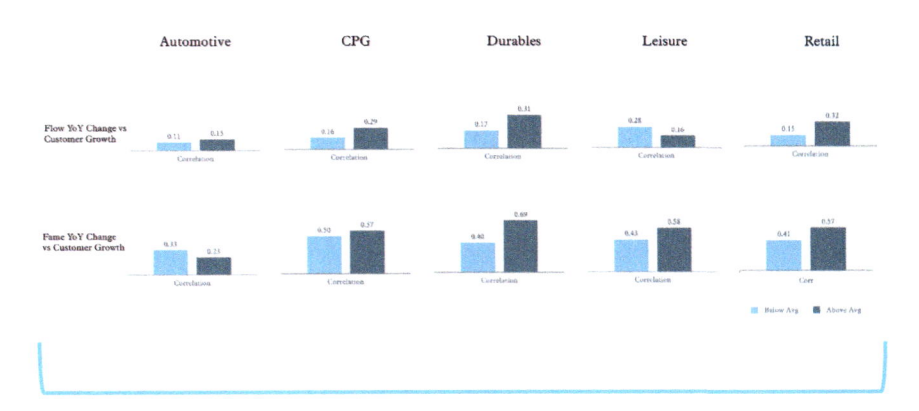

**Automotive**

Flow YoY Change vs Customer Growth: 0.11, 0.15

Fame YoY Change vs Customer Growth: 0.33, 0.25

**CPG**

Flow YoY Change vs Customer Growth: 0.16, 0.29

Fame YoY Change vs Customer Growth: 0.30, 0.37

**Durables**

Flow YoY Change vs Customer Growth: 0.12, 0.31

Fame YoY Change vs Customer Growth: 0.40, 0.69

**Leisure**

Flow YoY Change vs Customer Growth: 0.28, 0.16

Fame YoY Change vs Customer Growth: 0.43, 0.58

**Retail**

Flow YoY Change vs Customer Growth: 0.15, 0.32

Fame YoY Change vs Customer Growth: 0.41, 0.57

■ Below Avg ■ Above Avg

**CORRELATION BETWEEN NORMALIZED FAME X FLOW YOY GROWTH VERSUS CURRENT CUSTOMER YOY GROWTH IN % FOR EACH BIN LEVEL, BY CATEGORY**

## 3. The Fame x Flow Model is Consistent -- that Holds True Across Different Countries and Categories

The patterns we observe about Fame & Flow at a macro level were also observed for each of the three countries we investigated. From the table, it is clear that the correlation of Flow to the growth KPI is stronger as Fame increases from low to high. For Germany, for instance, the correlation more than triples from 0.17 to 0.42. Similarly for Fame, the correlation of Fame to the growth KPI increases as Flow increases. In the US, we see an increase in the correlation from 0.37 to 0.53 as Flow increases.

The patterns we observe about Fame & Flow at a macro level were also observed for across the categories we investigated. For Flow, there is an increase in the correlation between below average Fame and above average Fame. It holds in 4 of the 5 categories we examined. The only exception is QSR, the proxy for the Leisure category, where a different correlation pattern was observed. This points to a nuance in the model and may stem from the specific importance of proximity in QSR. Similarly, across categories for Fame, there is an increase in correlation with growth as we move from brands with below average Flow to brands with above average Flow. As with our investigation of Fame's effect on Flow, this notion of Flow's impact on Fame also holds true in 4 of the 5 categories we analyzed. Automotive was an outlier, where Fame's correlation to growth is lower for brands with above average Flow. Some categories with long purchase cycles such as Automotive require a nuanced approach in applying this model.

*"From the table, it is clear that the correlation of Flow to the growth KPI is stronger as Fame increases from low to high."*

*Fig.6 Relationship between normalized Fame x Flow YoY changes vs. YoY Customer Growth in percentage brand size.*

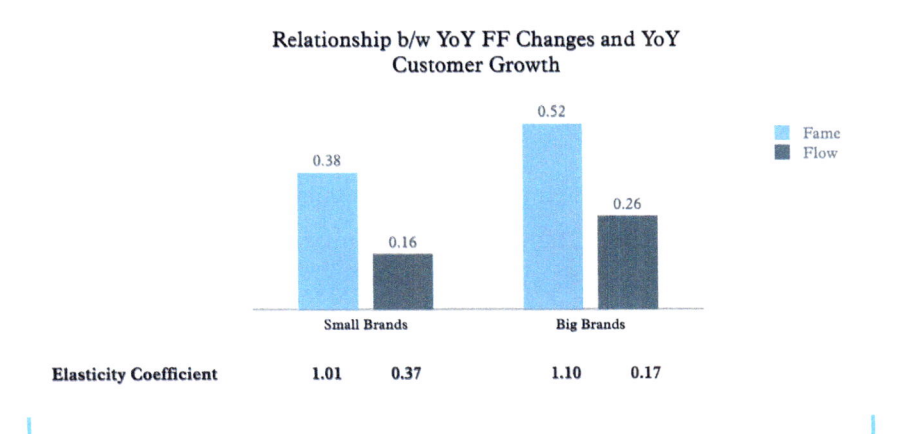

**Relationship b/w YoY FF Changes and YoY Customer Growth**

| | Small Brands | | Big Brands | |
|---|---|---|---|---|
| | Fame | Flow | Fame | Flow |
| Value | 0.38 | 0.16 | 0.52 | 0.26 |
| **Elasticity Coefficient** | 1.01 | 0.37 | 1.10 | 0.17 |

**RELATIONSHIP BETWEEN NORMALIZED FAME X FLOW YOY CHANGES VS YOY CUSTOMER GROWTH IN % BY BRAND SIZE**

### 4. Bigger Brands Benefit More in the World of Fame & Flow.

We asked ourselves the question, how does the size of a brand influence the relationship between being well-known (Fame), having a smooth customer journey (Flow), and overall performance (GKPI)?

Big brands, the ones that are already widely used and have higher market share (higher penetration), receive more benefit from both becoming even more well-known and liked (Fame) and having a smooth customer journey (Flow) compared to smaller brands. For these big brands, getting higher Fame has a 7 times bigger impact on how much they grow compared to improving their customer journey. On the other hand, for smaller brands, becoming more well-known has a 3 times bigger impact on growth than making the customer journey smoother. This does not mean that brands should invest solely in Fame over Flow. What it does mean is that brands need to really understand how Fame & Flow interact in their categories and markets.

Whilst the dynamics of Fame & Flow are somewhat category-nuanced and can vary based on brand size and point in its lifecycle, general principles still apply.

**All Good Research Should and Does Create New Lines of Inquiry**

As with all research, sometimes results raise interesting, new questions. We are committed to continuing to refine the Fame x Flow model and to find meaning or new rules that might be hidden in an exception.

**Statistical Analysis Commentary**

The research evaluated the strength of the relationship (if any) among variables Fame & Flow (and their constituent parts) and a KPI used as a proxy for growth (GKPI) through correlation analysis, scatter plots, and elasticity coefficients. The analysis was carried out across various categories, including Automotive, CPG, Durables, Retail, and Leisure, encompassing 185 brands in three major markets: the USA, Germany, and Australia.

For both correlation and scatterplots, we worked with normalized and non-normalized data. Normalizing the data allowed us to isolate the interrelationships among Fame, Flow, and GKPI without any brand size-related influence. We standardized the values relative to the dataset's minimum and maximum values. Standardization put disparate data points on similar scales and allowed us to compare and analyze the data more easily and fairly. Finally, we analyzed all relationships from different standpoints: First from an absolute standpoint, then through their year-over-year (YoY) differences.

Beyond individual assessments of Fame & Flow constituents, a focus was also placed on top-line correlations. Given that both Fame & Flow each have four constituent parts, we needed a way to arrive at a single aggregated value for Fame and for Flow. After several multivariate and univariate tests, we zeroed in on a simple average of normalized individual components Fs of Fame and Flow. More complicated approaches, like Principal Components Analysis, yielded the same ultimate conclusions about Fame & Flow. For the sake of simplicity, we thus chose the simple average of the constituent Fs to define Fame x Flow.

Correlation coefficients were used as the quantitative measure of the degree to which two variables exhibit a relationship or move in tandem. A coefficient close to 1 signifies a robust positive relationship, while a coefficient near -1 indicates a substantial negative relationship. Values nearing 0 suggest a limited or negligible relationship. Interpretation of correlation strength can vary, and common benchmarks based on the absolute value of correlation are as follows:

1. Weak Correlation (0.0 to 0.30): Generally considered weak, signifying a less pronounced or noticeable relationship between variables.
2. Moderate Correlation (0.30 to 0.50): Considered moderate or moderately strong, indicating a noticeable and moderate relationship.

3. Strong Correlation (0.50 to 1.00): Generally considered strong, suggesting a robust relationship where changes in one variable are predictably associated with changes in the other.

*"An R-square above 75% is indicative of a robust model, and our regression models range from 78% to 88%, reinforcing their robustness."*

In our study, we identify a moderate correlation (0.37) between Fame and GKPI, and a lower correlation (0.17) between Flow and GKPI. This indicates that at a top level across diverse brands and categories, there is considerable variation, and in scatter plots the relationship appears noisy. A brand in one category with high Fame is not guaranteed to have high GKPI.

However, this view does not account for heterogeneity across categories. A weak correlation does not mean statistically significant relationships do not exist. We find based on regression analysis of 24,000 observations that there are significant causal relationships between Fame x Flow and the KPI. These relationships were visualized through scatter plots.

Another method employed to quantify the impact of Fame & Flow on customer growth involved calculating the elasticity coefficient. Elasticity coefficients gauge the impact of a 1% change in an explanatory variable on the dependent variable. To do this, we created log-log regression with current customers as the dependent variable and Fame & Flow scores as explanatory variables. These analyses were conducted at both a top-line and category-specific level.

The validity and robustness of the elasticity coefficients derived from the log-log regression were assessed using three key metrics: R-square, confidence interval, and p-value. The R-square serves as a gauge to assess how accurately a prediction formula aligns with real-world observations. It provides insight into the effectiveness of the model by indicating how well it explains the variability in the actual data. An R-square above 75% is indicative of a robust model, and our regression models range from 78% to 88%, reinforcing their robustness. Additionally, a confidence interval layer is introduced, providing a range of values within which the true parameter is anticipated to fall with a specified level of confidence. For instance, a 90% confidence interval for the average percentage change in brand growth resulting from a 1% change in Fame might be reported as 1.32 ± 0.015%. This denotes 90% confidence that the true impact of a 1% change in Fame on brand growth lies within the range of 1.31% to 1.34%.

Finally, to evaluate the individual variable significance, we compared the variable's p-value in comparison to the significance level (a), set at 0.01. A p-value below "a" rejects the null hypothesis, indicating that the explanatory variable significantly impacts the dependent variable. In this study, nearly all Fame and Flow metrics exhibit significantly low p-values, even lower than 0.0001, indicating that they are highly significant explanatory variables.

# INDEX

Hopkins, Claude. *Scientific Advertising*. Chelsea House, 1980.

Weir, Peter. *The Truman Show*. Paramount Pictures, 1998.

Ambler, Tim. *Marketing and the Bottom Line*. Financial Times/Prentice Hall, 2000, 2001. p. 18.

Feldwick, Paul. *The Anatomy of Humbug: How to Think Differently About Advertising*. Troubador Publishing Ltd, 2015.

"Fearless Girl." State Street Global Advisors, created by McCann New York, 2017, sculpture.

"15 Minutes Could Save You 15% or More on Car Insurance." Geico, 2006, TV commercial.

"Just Do It." Nike, created by Wieden+Kennedy, 1988, TV commercial.

"Real Beauty." Dove, created by Ogilvy & Mather, 2004, TV commercial.

"Belong Anywhere." Airbnb, created by TBWA\Chiat\Day, 2014, TV commercial.

"Extreme Sports Community." Red Bull, created by Kastner & Partners, 2012, TV commercial.

Sharp, Byron. *How Brands Grow: What Marketers Don't Know*. OUP Australia and New Zealand, 2010.

"I'm Lovin' It." McDonald's, created by DDB Worldwide, 2003, TV commercial.

"Wassup." Budweiser, created by DDB Worldwide, 1999, TV commercial.

"Like a Girl." Always, created by Leo Burnett, 2014, TV commercial.

"What Drives Advertising Effectiveness? Mark Ritson's 10 Key Factors - Hub." Hub., 12 July 2023, www.hubagency.co.uk/what-drives-advertising-effectiveness-mark-ritsons-10-key-factors.

Binet, Les, and Peter Field. *The Long and the Short of It: Balancing Short and Long-Term Marketing Strategies*. IPA, 2013.

"System One's Industry Studies." System One, 2024.

Simkin, Mikhail V., and Vwani Roychowdhury. "A Mathematical Theory of Fame." Journal of Statistical Physics, vol. 151, no. 1-2, 12 Jan. 2013, pp. 319-328.

Pais, Abraham, Maurice Jacob, David I. Olive, and Michael F. Atiyah, editors. *Paul Dirac: The Man and His Work*. Cambridge University Press, 2005.

Author, No. "Dirac, Einstein and Physics – Physics World." Physics World, 2 Jan. 2019, physicsworld.com/a/dirac-einstein-and-physics.

Schulman, Eric. "Can Fame Be Measured Quantitatively?" Annals of Improbable Research, vol. 5, no. 3, 1999, p. 16.

ITV Fame Ratings, 2005. BBH, 2005.

Feldwick, Paul. *Why Does the Pedlar Sing? What Creativity Really Means in Advertising*. Matador, 2021.

Kahneman, Daniel. *Thinking, Fast and Slow*. Farrar, Straus and Giroux, 2011.

Protheroe, Jonny, et al. Decoding Decisions: Making Sense of the Messy Middle.

www.thinkwithgoogle.com/_qs/documents/9998/Decoding_Decisions_The_Messy_Middle_of_Purchase_Behavior.pdf.
Creswell, Julie. "Overstock Will Rebrand as Bed Bath & Beyond Online." *The New York Times*, 28 June 2023, www.nytimes.com/2023/06/28/business/overstock-bed-bath-beyond.html.

"Ogilvy Paris Presents a Not-So-Classical Date With Tinder and Radio France's Musical Groups." adsofbrands.net, adsofbrands.net/en/news/ogilvy-paris-presents-a-not-so-classical-date-with-tinder-and-radio-france-s-musical-groups/3240.
"Fallout Campaign." Amazon Prime Video, created by Kilter Films, 2024, TV commercial.

"Rexona, Primeros Pasos." Initiative, 2022.

"Campaign of the Week: FitChix." Contagious, www.contagious.com/news-and-views/campaign-of-the-week-produce-brand-prints-chickens-step-counts-on-eggs-as-proof-of-welfare.

Collins, Marcus. "Twitter's Rebrand Is a Cautionary Lesson for Marketers. Here's Why." *Forbes*, 31 July 2023, www.forbes.com/sites/marcuscollins/2023/07/30/the-real-lesson-to-be-learned-from-twitters-rebrand/?sh=1fe9d2211fd2.

"History of the MICHELIN Guide." MICHELIN Guide, guide.michelin.com/th/en/history-of-the-michelin-guide-th.

"Real Beauty." Dove, created by Ogilvy & Mather, 2004, TV commercial.

"NRMA Insurance Cricket Covers: How Emotional Connection Scored a Brand Win." NRMA Insurance, created by Thinkerbell and Initiative, 2022, TV commercial.

153

Berger, Jonah. *Contagious: Why Things Catch On*. Simon & Schuster, 2013.

Roy, Jessica. "After Two Dates, Her Designer Shoes Went Missing." *The New York Times*, 7 Sept. 2023, www.nytimes.com/2023/09/06/style/tiktok-missing-tabi-shoes.html. "Nike Seizes Controversy by the Bullish Horns." *Forbes*, 12 Sept. 2018, www.forbes.com/sites/alapshah/2018/09/12/a-social-media-and-sentiment-analysis-of-nike-what-does-it-mean-for-future-purchase-intent/?sh=5cdba0882f45.

"LEGO Piece Garden Campaign." Initiative, 2023. Media Partner: It's Nice That. Production by It's Nice That and Anyways. PR by Mischief. Artists: Charlotte Mei, Alec Doherty, Ciarán Birch.

"Aperol's SEO Strategy During the COVID-19 Pandemic." *Search Engine Land*, 2023, https://searchengineland.com/adapting-your-seo-strategy-to-soften-the-impact-of-covid-19-on-organic-traffic-330938. Accessed 27 June 2024.

"Aperol's Shift to Direct-to-Consumer Marketing During the Pandemic." Digital Marketing Institute, 2023, https://digitalmarketinginstitute.com/resources/reports/the-future-of-marketing-after-covid-19. Accessed 27 June 2024.

"Importance of SEO During COVID-19 Pandemic." BrightEdge, 2023, https://www.brightedge.com/resources/webinars/importance-of-seo-during-covid-19-pandemic. Accessed 27 June 2024.

Spangler, Todd. "Tubi Freaks Out Super Bowl Viewers With 'Interface Interruption' Ad." *Variety*, 13 Feb. 2023, variety.com/2023/digital/news/tubi-super-bowl-ad-channel-change-interface-interruption-1235521119.

"Ring, Memorial Day Moment of Truth." Initiative, 2023.

Morris, Chris. "McDonald's to Offer 'Free Fries Friday' Through the End of 2023." *Fortune*, 24 Oct. 2023, fortune.com/2023/10/24/mcdonalds-free-french-fries-friday-app.

TurboTax® Official Site: File Taxes Online, Tax Filing Made Easy." TurboTax, Intuit, 1993, https://turbotax.intuit.com.

"Artefacta's Mom Translator: A Case Study in Facilitating the Path to Purchase." Artefacta, 2024.

Schultz, E.J. "Telecom Brand Skinny Wins Cannes Lions 2023 Radio & Audio Grand Prix." *Ad Age*, 20 June 2023, https://adage.com/article/special-report-cannes-lions/telecom-brand-skinny-wins-cannes-lions-2023-radio-audio-grand-prix/2500491.

Gilead Sciences: In the Deep | WARC. www.warc.com/content/paywall/article/warc-cases/gilead-sciences-in-the-deep/en-gb/149876.

Griff, Zach. "Delta SkyMiles Change Saga: Improvements Made to Medallion Status and Sky Club Lounge Access." *The Points Guy*, 24 Oct. 2023, thepointsguy.com/news/delta-skymiles-changes-update.

"Spotify Wrapped." Spotify, 2016, https://www.spotify.com/us/wrapped/.

41% of Current Industry Measurement Metrics Do Not Reflect Marketing Effectiveness | DMA. dma.org.uk/press-release/41-of-current-industry-measurement-metrics-do-not-reflect-marketing-effectiveness.

Whittaker, Ian. "Speak the Language of the CFO and CEO to Make Investment Case for Marketing." *Campaign US*, 13 Nov. 2023, www.campaignlive.com/article/speak-language-cfo-ceo-investment-case-marketing/1846464.

IPA | Marketing Is an Investment. ipa.co.uk/knowledge/publications-reports/marketing-is-an-investment.

Svendsen, John, and John Svendsen. "It Works for Coca-Cola and Google and It Can Work for You Too: The 70-20-10 Rule - the Media Leader." The Media Leader - 100% Media: News Analysis, Opinion, Trends, Data & Jobs, 20 Nov. 2012, the-media-leader.com/it-works-for-coca-cola-and-google-and-it-can-work-for-you-too-the-70-20-10-rule.

Allianz Case Study, "Can Marketing Experimentation Become Your Superpower?" Bain, 28 Sept. 2023, www.bain.com/insights/can-marketing-experimentation-become-your-superpower.

Printed in Great Britain
by Amazon